Mary Queen *of* Scots

AN ILLUSTRATED LIFE

.1. The savety of y[e] Q. of Scott is first to be consydered, y[t] by no practise she shuld be conveyed out of y[e] realme.

.2. She shuld be discretly treated w[ith] to know whyther she will be contented to have hir cause examyned, and by whom, and in what maner. and furder to declare what she will assure of y[e] Q. Ma[jes]ty, so as hir hir Ma[jes]ty may consyder of y[e] reasonablenes of hir demand, and to [use] therin as shall pertayne to honor.

.3. If y[e] Erle of Murraye and y[e] nobilite of Scotland in y[e] name of y[e] prynce whom they have receaved for thir kyng, shall requir to have the causes of thir procedyng ageynst the Quene heard by hir Ma[jes]ty, it is reason to yeld thereunto.

Note y[t] it appereth honorable and mete for y[e] Q. [well]? as Quene of England, to take uppon hir, y[e] hearyng decydyng and determynyng of any controversy moved for y[e] crown of Scotland for y[t] of ancient right it appartineth to y[e] crown of England, as by multitude of records, examples, and presidents may be proved.
Note also y[t] it is necessary e proffitable, at this tyme for y[e] Q. Ma[jes]ty to entremedle herin.
.1. first for y[t] y[e] Q. of Scott hath hertofor openly made challenge to y[e] crown of england, not as a second person aft[er] y[e] Q. Ma[jes]ty, but afore hir.
.2. secondly it is proffitable for y[e] realm of england, to have an alliance w[ith] scotland, and lykewise for scotland, to be out of bondage of france, and allyed w[ith] england. for these ij beinge frendly and peacibly joyned w[ith] feland getud, may sorely preserve them sorted w[ith] good gouinm[en]t, from y[e] malice of frate, and y[e] rest of christendom.
.3. Thirdly, by coniunction of these ij in band ageynst y[e] usurped power of Roome the cause of religion shall also be [...]

Mary Queen of Scots

AN ILLUSTRATED LIFE

SUSAN DORAN

THE BRITISH LIBRARY

In memory of my sister,
Judy, 1947–2004

First published in 2007 by
The British Library
96 Euston Road
London NW1 2DB

Text © 2007 Susan Doran
Illustrations © 2007 The
British Library and other
named copyright holders

British Library Cataloguing
in Publication Data
A catalogue record for
this book is available from
The British Library

ISBN 0 7123 4916 2
ISBN 978 0 7123 4916 1

Designed and typeset
in Scala and Scala Sans
by Andrew Barron @
thextension

Printed in Hong Kong by
South Sea International
Press

The British Library would
like to thank all copyright
holders for permission to
reproduce material and
illustrations. While every
effort has been made to
trace and acknowledge
copyright holders, we
would like to apologize for
any errors or omissions.

Front jacket illustration:
*Portrait of Mary Queen of
Scots. c.*1610 (1578?) after
Nicholas Hilliard (National
Portrait Gallery, London)

Jacket background: Extract
from Mary's subscription
to the Bond of Association
made on 5 January 1585
(British Library, Additional
MS 48027, f. 249, enlarged)

Back jacket illustration:
Woodcut of Mary's Execution
from Adam Blackwood's
*Histoire et Martyre de la
Royne d'Escosse*, Paris, 1589
(British Library, G1745)

Page 1 illustration: *Portrait
of Mary Queen of Scots.
c.*1569 by an unknown
artist (The Blairs Museum,
Aberdeen)

Page 2 illustration:
Extract from notes by
Sir William Cecil in which
he justifies putting Mary
on trial, May 1568
(British Library, Cotton
Caligula C. I, f. 98)

Pages 10–11 and 13
illustrations by
Cedric Knight

Acknowledgements
I would like to thank
Dr Pauline Croft and Jim
Gallagher for reading the
text and making very useful
suggestions. I am also
indebted to the publications
department at the British
Library, particularly Trish
Burgess, Kathy Houghton
and Charlotte Lochhead,
for their invaluable
assistance and
commitment to this
project.

Author's note
The size of certain
documents has been
adjusted to aid legibility,
and the spelling of all
quotations in the text has
been modernized. The
Scottish form of Stewart
has been preferred here to
Stuart, which is the French
spelling. (In the sixteenth
century the French
alphabet had no 'w'.)
Mary of Guise has been
called by her French name,
Marie de Guise, in order
to avoid confusion with
her daughter.

Contents

Introduction

Mary Queen of Scots has been the subject of innumerable plays, poems, songs, operas, films, novels and biographies. It is not difficult to see why. The first twenty years of her life were packed with dramatic incident, including her flight to France, widowhood at an early age, the murder of her secretary and second husband, her abduction and rape by a third, and finally captivity and escape from a remote castle in the Highlands of Scotland. Her last eighteen years as a prisoner in England, while certainly quieter, were nonetheless marked by conspiracy and intrigue; and her execution, in February 1587, provided a fitting final scene to a drama that had seen her fall tragically from power and splendour into confinement and despair. For well over half her life, moreover, she was the rival of Queen Elizabeth I of England, a ruler of a very different temperament and history. Their relationship can easily be portrayed as a clash between contrasts, a battle between yin and yang, as well as a struggle to the death between competitors for the English throne. Not surprisingly, therefore, creative writers as diverse as Friedrich Schiller, Sir Walter Scott, Robert Burns, Alphonse de Lamartine, Algernon Swinburne, John Drinkwater, Jean Plaidy, Margaret Irwin and Liz Lochhead (and, indeed, many more) have turned their hand to capturing the excitement and tragic quality of Mary's life.

Mary is also an enigma. Both during her lifetime and thereafter, men and women have puzzled over her character, questioned the depth of her religious piety, and argued over the extent of her involvement in the murder of her second husband, Henry, Lord Darnley. Was Mary a committed Catholic, determined to undo the Protestant settlement in Scotland, as the Protestant preacher John Knox claimed? Were the Casket Letters genuine billets-doux and sonnets addressed to her lover, the Earl of Bothwell, during the last months of her marriage to Darnley, which, according to George Buchanan, exposed 'the conspiracy, device and execution' of 'Darnley's horrible murder by the said Queen, his wife'? Or were they actually forgeries, as a number of historians have contended? Was Mary the devious schemer who conspired with English Catholic fanatics and foreign rulers to assassinate Queen Elizabeth and seize her throne, or was she an innocent victim, stitched up by Elizabeth's ministers Sir William Cecil (later Lord Burghley) and Sir Francis Walsingham?

These questions have never been resolved, and never will be, partly because Mary's life was originally the property of polemical writers. The contemporary Scottish Protestants John Knox and George Buchanan vilified her in their histories of the period because they hated her religion and sought to justify her overthrow as Queen of Scotland. Predictably, Catholic writers, such as her

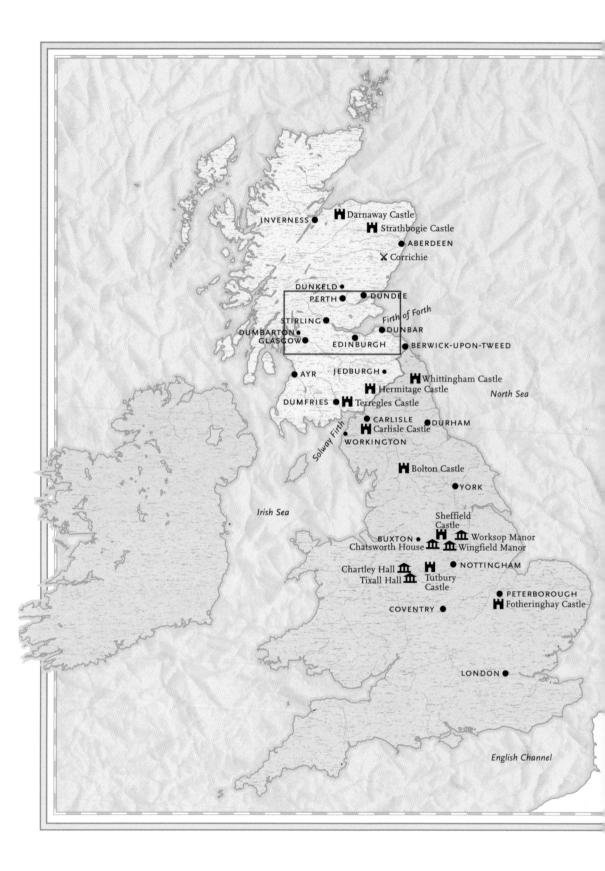

INVERNESS ●

🏰 Darnaway Castle

🏰 Strathbogie Castle

● ABERDEEN

✕ Corrichie

DUNKELD ●
PERTH ●   ● DUNDEE

STIRLING ●   *Firth of Forth*
DUMBARTON ●   ● DUNBAR
GLASGOW ●
                EDINBURGH ●   ● BERWICK-UPON-TWEED

● AYR   JEDBURGH ●

                                🏰 Whittingham Castle
                    🏰 Hermitage Castle   *North Sea*

DUMFRIES ●   🏰 Terregles Castle

                ● CARLISLE
            🏰 Carlisle Castle   ● DURHAM
Solway Firth
        WORKINGTON ●

                🏰 Bolton Castle

Irish Sea   ● YORK

                        Sheffield
                        Castle
        BUXTON ●   🏛 🏛 Worksop Manor
    Chatsworth House 🏛 🏛 Wingfield Manor

    Chartley Hall 🏛 🏰   ● NOTTINGHAM
    Tixall Hall 🏛   Tutbury
                        Castle
                                ● PETERBOROUGH
        COVENTRY ●   🏰 Fotheringhay Castle

                        LONDON ●

English Channel

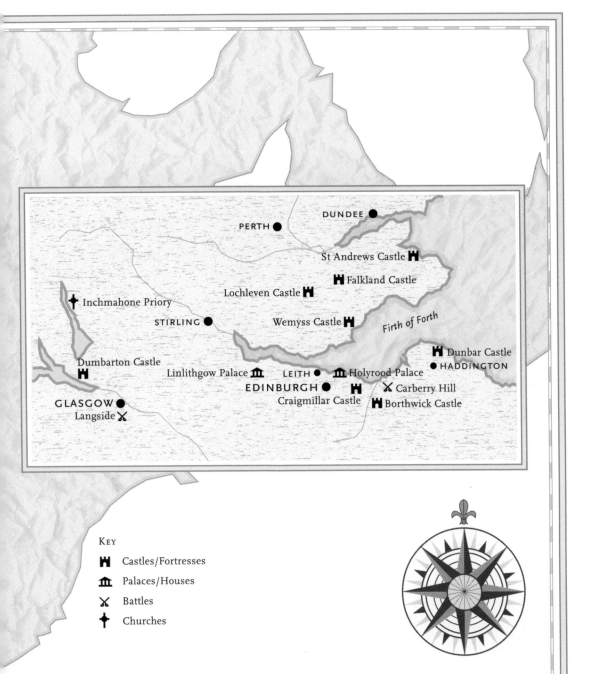

KEY

- **Castles/Fortresses**
- **Palaces/Houses**
- **Battles**
- **Churches**

DUNDEE

PERTH

St Andrews Castle

Falkland Castle

Lochleven Castle

Inchmahone Priory

STIRLING

Wemyss Castle

Firth of Forth

Dumbarton Castle

Linlithgow Palace

LEITH

Holyrood Palace

Dunbar Castle

HADDINGTON

EDINBURGH

Carberry Hill

GLASGOW

Craigmillar Castle

Borthwick Castle

Langside

Places Relating to the Life of Mary Queen of Scots

contemporaries John Leslie and Adam Blackwood, sprang to her defence, protesting her innocence in the murder of Darnley and plots against Elizabeth. As much as they would like to, historians cannot entirely escape the influence of these works; it is mainly through John Knox's *History of the Reformation in Scotland*, for example, that they have access to Mary's famous interviews with the fiery preacher. Furthermore, historians are heavily dependent on the reports of ambassadors to the French and Scottish courts for their knowledge of the queen, and these men were not impartial observers, but rather reflected the religious divide at the time of writing.

Mary has few achievements to her name. Even worse, during her personal rule Scotland slipped first into factional unrest and then into civil war. Indeed, it could be argued that her only enduring legacy to history was the birth of her son, who as James VI of Scotland and I of England, created the union of the two crowns. Nevertheless, Mary was immensely influential during her lifetime, not so much because of her deeds, but because of her dynastic relationship to the Guises in France and the Tudors in England. As a result of this family connection, her presence dominated Elizabethan political life and became the obsession of English statesmen until her death. It is because of this contemporary significance, as well as the compelling story of her life and the controversies it has provoked, that Mary deserves her place in history.

The Tudors and Stewarts

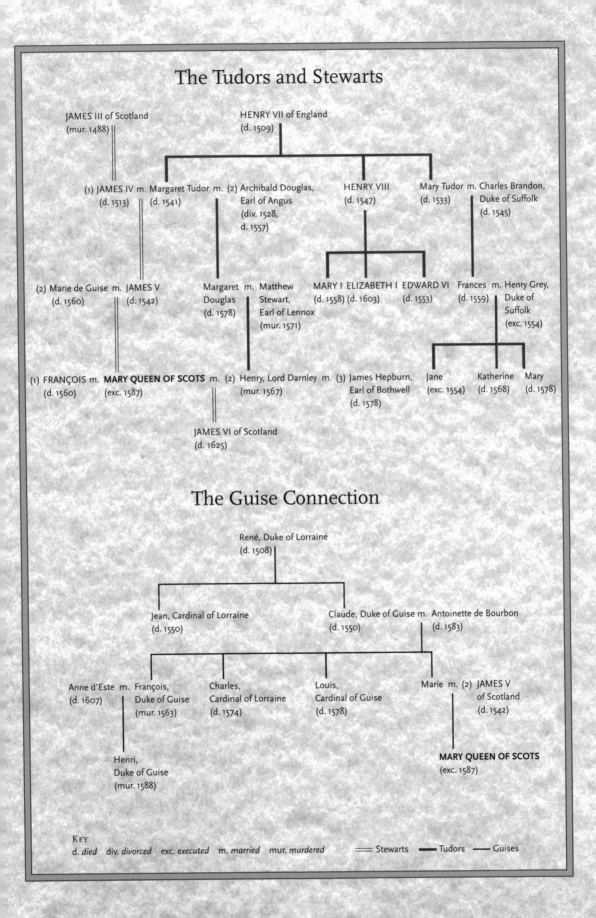

JAMES III of Scotland
(mur. 1488)

HENRY VII of England
(d. 1509)

(1) JAMES IV m. Margaret Tudor m. (2) Archibald Douglas,
(d. 1513)   (d. 1541)   Earl of Angus
                                              (div. 1528,
                                              d. 1557)

HENRY VIII
(d. 1547)

Mary Tudor m. Charles Brandon,
(d. 1533)   Duke of Suffolk
                   (d. 1545)

(2) Marie de Guise m. JAMES V
(d. 1560)   (d. 1542)

Margaret m. Matthew
Douglas   Stewart,
(d. 1578)   Earl of Lennox
                 (mur. 1571)

MARY I   ELIZABETH I   EDWARD VI
(d. 1558) (d. 1603)   (d. 1553)

Frances m. Henry Grey,
(d. 1559)   Duke of
                 Suffolk
                 (exc. 1554)

(1) FRANÇOIS m. **MARY QUEEN OF SCOTS** m. (2) Henry, Lord Darnley m. (3) James Hepburn,
(d. 1560)   (exc. 1587)   (mur. 1567)   Earl of Bothwell
                                                                               (d. 1578)

Jane   Katherine   Mary
(exc. 1554)   (d. 1568)   (d. 1578)

JAMES VI of Scotland
(d. 1625)

The Guise Connection

René, Duke of Lorraine
(d. 1508)

Jean, Cardinal of Lorraine
(d. 1550)

Claude, Duke of Guise m. Antoinette de Bourbon
(d. 1550)   (d. 1583)

Anne d'Este m. François,
(d. 1607)   Duke of Guise
                   (mur. 1563)

Charles,
Cardinal of Lorraine
(d. 1574)

Louis,
Cardinal of Guise
(d. 1578)

Marie m. (2) JAMES V
                 of Scotland
                 (d. 1542)

Henri,
Duke of Guise
(mur. 1588)

MARY QUEEN OF SCOTS
(exc. 1587)

KEY
d. *died*   div. *divorced*   exc. *executed*   m. *married*   mur. *murdered*   ═══ Stewarts   ━━━ Tudors   ━━━ Guises

Lau 1552 An mois de Juillet
1552

CHAPTER ONE

Early Life in Scotland and France
1542–1558

O N   T H E   F E A S T   of the Immaculate Conception, 8 December 1542, a baby girl was born at Linlithgow Palace in West Lothian. Her father was King James V of Scotland, and her mother his queen consort, Marie de Guise. Marie, the daughter of the Duke of Guise and a member of the powerful French family known as the House of Lorraine, had become James's wife in 1538, a year after the death of her first husband, the Duke of Longueville. In coming to Scotland to marry the king, Marie had made great personal sacrifices, for she had left behind in France not only her parents and brothers, but also, more heart-wrenchingly, her two-year-old son. This second marriage brought her little happiness; apart from homesickness, Marie worried for eighteen months about her failure to conceive. Then, in April 1541, the two sons she had borne James died within hours of each other, the younger one being only a few days old. Given the day of her birth and the name of her mother, it is not surprising that the new royal baby was baptized Mary.

OPPOSITE
Portrait of Mary Aged Nine and a Half, 1552 by Jean Clouet. The inscription on this red and black chalk drawing states that it was produced in July 1552, the same month and year as the drawing of the dauphin (see page 29).
(Musée Condé, Chantilly)

Portrait of Henry VIII of England, c.1536–7 by an unknown artist. Henry was Mary's great uncle, and defeated her father at the battle of Solway Moss in 1542. From then on his policy was to force the Scots to agree to a marriage between Mary and his son, Edward. (National Portrait Gallery, London)

The baptism ceremony was a low-key affair, and is presumed to have taken place at St Michael's Church, next to Linlithgow Palace, shortly after the birth. James V did not attend. He had visited his wife on 4 December during the last stage of her pregnancy, but was at that time in a state of near nervous collapse and he moved restlessly on, first to Edinburgh and then to his favourite castle of Falkland in Fife, where he took to his bed. When learning of the safe delivery of his daughter, he famously (but possibly mythically) said, 'Adieu, farewell, it [the crown of Scotland] cam wi' a lass, it will gang wi' a lass'. The first lass was the daughter of Robert the Bruce through whom the Stewarts had secured the Scottish throne in 1371. A week later, the thirty-one-year-old king was dead.

James's illness, though possibly not his death, was brought on by grief, anger and despair at his army's recent defeat at the hands of the English. On 24 November 1542 some 17,000 of his men had been routed by a much smaller but well-disciplined English force that had ambushed them at Solway Moss by the River Esk. Few of the Scots were actually killed by the English, but around 1,200 were captured, including twenty-three of the most important nobles and lairds. Although this defeat was by no means catastrophic and hardly threatened Scotland's independence, it was deeply mortifying for James, who for at least a decade had felt a strong sense of rivalry with his uncle King Henry VIII. Perhaps the knowledge that the Scottish captives would be held hostage and paraded through the streets of London was just too painful for him to bear.

James's death on 14 December 1542 left his
daughter as Queen of Scotland at the age of six
days. She was reported to be a very weak child
and 'not expected to live',[1] but in fact she
turned out to be one of the healthiest of the
king's offspring (he had about nine illegitimate
children). Given her age, a regency was
inevitable, and after a brief power struggle
James Hamilton, 2nd Earl of Arran and heir
presumptive to the throne, was appointed
Governor of Scotland during the queen's
minority. Unquestionably, Arran had a difficult
job on his hands in governing the kingdom,
and not the least of his many problems was
Henry VIII's determination to exploit the
political weakness of the Scottish realm and
unite it to England. The kings of Scotland had
long been a thorn in Henry's side: James V's
father had launched an invasion in 1512 as an
ally of the French king, while James himself
had consistently been pro-French and
unwilling to follow directions from Henry.
Now that he was dead, Henry saw an excellent
opportunity to end Scotland's independence
by arranging a match between the young
Queen Mary and his own son and heir, Prince
Edward, then aged five. Such a dynastic union
would enhance England's security and bolster
Henry's prestige. It would prevent Mary – and
Scotland – from falling into the hands of
another European dynasty. Perhaps most
important of all, with Scotland confirmed as
an ally, it would leave Henry free to pursue
his plan of invading France without having
concerns about the defence of his northern
border.

ABOVE
*Engraving of James
Hamilton, 2nd Earl of Arran,
c.1823, from Lodge's British
Portraits.* Arran was next in
line to the throne of
Scotland until Mary's son
was born in 1566. Acting as
regent for Mary until 1554,
he made an alliance with
Henri II of France in 1548,
agreeing to Mary's
marriage to the dauphin.
As a reward, Henri
awarded him the title of
Duke of Châtelherault and
the Order of St Michael,
which he is wearing around
his neck.
(British Library, 10804.k.13)

OVERLEAF
*Portrait of James VI of
Scotland and Marie de
Guise,* 1895 copy of a
sixteenth-century painting
by an unknown artist.
Mary's parents married in
1538, and their daughter
was born on 8 December
1542, just six days before
her father's death.
(Falkland Palace/
Bridgeman Art Library)

IACOBVS QVINTVS SCOTTORVM REX
ANNO ÆTATIS SVE
28

MARIA.LOTHORINGIA.ILLIVS.IN.SECVNDIS.NVP
TIIS.VXOR.ANNO ÆTATIS SVE.Z 4 :⸱

Under pressure from Henry, Governor Arran agreed to pursue an English marriage for his young queen. The Scottish parliament gave its consent too, no doubt because of the military supremacy of England, though its members might well have preferred Mary to wed an absentee foreign prince rather than the scion of an ambitious Scottish noble family. However, from the start there was also strong opposition to the match amongst the pro-French party in Scotland, headed by Cardinal David Beaton, and throughout the early summer of 1543 many other Scots began to doubt its wisdom as they realized that a dynastic union with its stronger neighbour put at risk Scotland's independence. To ensure its preservation, the Scottish commissioners who negotiated the marriage treaty were adamant that Mary should not reside in England until the marriage took place, and that Scotland's liberties and independence would be preserved afterwards. On 1 July 1543 the English king and Scottish commissioners signed the Treaties of Greenwich, which approved the terms for the marriage and accepted that Mary would remain in Scotland until she reached ten years of age.

While these discussions about her future were taking place, Mary was living with her mother in the large, Italianate palace of Linlithgow, a few hours west of Edinburgh. It was to Linlithgow that Henry VIII's ambassador, Sir Ralph Sadler, went in March 1543 to view the baby unclothed and check that she was not deformed or unhealthy, or, in other words, would live to make a suitable bride for Edward.

Sadler was suitably impressed, reporting that she was 'as goodly a child as I have seen of her age, and as like to live'. Immediately after the marriage treaty was signed, Marie de Guise was determined to take her daughter from Linlithgow to the fortress of Stirling (which was part of her dowry) because she was afraid that the English would try to abduct the child and carry her off to England. Unlike Linlithgow, Stirling had a good defensive position, situated as it was on top of a steep crag and far from the sea. On 27 July 1543 Marie and her seven-month-old daughter left for Stirling escorted by 2,500 horsemen and a thousand heavily armed men on foot, while the carts carrying their possessions extended for almost a mile.

OPPOSITE
Letter from Sir Ralph Sadler to Henry VIII, dated 23 March 1543, recounting his meeting with Marie de Guise and his first impression of Mary as a baby. He reports (fourteen lines down) Marie telling him that Arran had said the child was not likely to live:

'"...but you shall see," quoth she, "whether he saieth true or not"; and therewith she caused me to go with her to the chamber where the child was, and showed her unto me, and also caused the nurse to unwrap her out of her clothes, that I might see her naked. I assure your majesty, it is as goodly a child as I have seen of her age, and as like to live, with the grace of God.'

(British Library, Additional MS 32650, f. 74, enlarged)

to be suerlie as yo[r] highnes therfore coulde not suspect
her but rather doubted not she woulde applye to that
shulde be for her honor and the most suretie and benefite
of her daughter wherbie if she maryed it wolde she myght
repent and her selfe rest w[i]t[h] yo[r] Ma[tie] and woulde the same
myght be in greate daungier She confessed the
same and wysshed to god that she were in yo[r] Ma[ties]
handes for she sayth it hath been seldome seen that
theyr of a realme shulde be in the custodie of him that
claymeth the succession of the same, as she sayd the
governor is nowe establysshed by p[ar]lament the second
p[er]son of this realme and if her daughter faylie lookyth
to be kyng of the same And yet she she sayd that
the chylde was not lyke to lyve but yo[u] shall see god
she wolud[?] the same true or not And therto she
caused me to go w[i]t[h] her in to the chamber where
the chylde was, and shewed her unto me and also
caused the Nurice to unwrapp her oute of her
clowtes that I myght see her naked I assure yo[r]
Ma[tie] it is as goodlie a chylde as I have seen of
her age and as lyke to lyve w[i]t[h] the grace of
god Qub when I had seen the chylde and retorned
to the saide Donag[ier]s as is aforesaide I toke
my leave and retorned hither to Edinburghe this
same where as yet neyther the Governor nor any
of the noble men of Scotland but are all disp[er]sid
downe [?] man at his owne howse abrode in the
countrey It is saide the Governor and many of
them wolbe here this feast[?] I woll do what I
to dyscypher theyr meanyng toward yo[r] Ma[tie] if
is it be true that the saide Donag[ier] sayth there
there is greate dyssimulation amongst them

This mornyng I receyved a lre from Mr Poynts
yor Lordshipe shall receyve herinclosed And thus
John Chrilitine pserve yor good Lordshippe in long
healthe and honor ffrom Edenburgh the xvijth of Aug

At the despche herof I am al
redy to take my horse to ryde to th...
to speke wt the olde quene who hath
sent for me as I wrot in my last l
to the kynge mat At my returne yor
Lordshippes may be sure I woll
advertise the rest of her sendinge
me / and vogar for saythe accordingly

yor Lordshippes
f mannde

[signature]

Sadler had been informed that the move was intended simply to make the royal family more comfortable in the spacious and luxurious apartments at Stirling. He was taken again to view the child in early August 1543, and reported back to Henry that she was 'a right fair and goodly child as any that I have seen for her age.'[2] But despite these reassurances and the fact that the Treaties of Greenwich were ratified in late August 1543, Henry's matrimonial project was in severe difficulties. Indeed, only a few days after the ratification Arran made his peace with Cardinal Beaton and defected from the English cause. Shortly afterwards, on Sunday 9 September, in a ceremony designed to convey Scotland's determination to retain its independence, Mary was publicly crowned and anointed queen in the Chapel Royal of Stirling Castle. In the procession Arran, as Scotland's premier nobleman, carried the royal crown; Matthew Stewart, 4th Earl of Lennox (also of royal blood) held the sceptre, while Archibald Campbell, the 4th Earl of Argyll (the most powerful of the Scottish lords) bore the sword of state. Beaton performed the ceremony and held the heavy imperial crown over the nine-month-old infant, who was of course far too small to wear it. Mary was understandably unaware of the solemnity of the occasion, and in fact bawled throughout. The festivities continued with banquets, masques, dramatic interludes and dancing held in the Great Hall at Stirling.

The coronation not only affirmed Mary's status as an independent monarch, but also marked the rejection of the English alliance. The main

OPPOSITE
Letter from Sir Ralph Sadler to the Privy Council, dated 6 August 1543. Written by a clerk, but with a postscript in Sadler's own hand, the letter reports that he is ready to ride to Stirling to speak with 'the old queen who hath sent for me' (Marie de Guise). He informed the king about her summons in his previous letter, and now he tells the council that on his return from Stirling he will 'advertise the cause of her sending for me'. At his meeting with Marie, she tried to reassure him that she still favoured the English marriage. She also took Sadler for a second viewing of Mary so that he could again see how healthy the child was. (British Library, Additional MS 32651, f. 204)

ABOVE
Stirling Castle, Scotland, where Mary was moved for her protection in July 1543. This great fortress remained her main place of residence until she was taken to France. On 9 September 1543 she was crowned in Stirling Castle's Chapel Royal. (© Crown Copyright, 2006, Historic Scotland Images)

participants in the ceremony were those noblemen hostile to the English alliance, while pro-English nobles stayed away. It therefore came as no surprise when, on 11 December 1543, the Scottish parliament formally repudiated the Treaties of Greenwich, reaffirmed the Auld Alliance with France, and appointed Beaton as chancellor of the realm. Humiliated and enraged by the failure of his diplomacy, Henry turned to military aggression, and in April 1544 he ordered his brother-in-law Edward Seymour, Earl of Hertford, to cross into Scotland and 'put all to fire and sword', to burn and sack Edinburgh and Leith, and 'extend like extremities and destructions' to the towns and villages in Fife (the main arable region of Scotland) so that 'there may remain forever a perpetual memory of the vengeance of God lightened upon [them] for their falsehood and disloyalty'.[3] Henry's aim was twofold: revenge and a 'Rough Wooing' to enforce the marriage of Mary to his son.

In May 1544, with an army of some 15,000 men, Hertford advanced into Scotland and devastated the eastern Lowlands. He was unable to capture Edinburgh Castle, but otherwise carried out his instructions efficiently. For safety Mary was temporarily removed to Dunkeld, one of the main approaches to the Highlands, some thirty miles northwards. However, she soon returned to Stirling, since Hertford's punitive raid was short-lived. His troops were withdrawn to participate in the invasion of France, but they returned in September 1545 to renew the scorched-earth policy just in time to burn the newly cut harvest in the Tweed valley. The final year of Henry's reign, 1546, saw a lull in the fighting in Scotland. Financially exhausted by his military efforts in France and Scotland, Henry and the French king, François I, signed the Peace Treaty of Camp, which comprehended Scotland as France's ally.

In spite of the devastation in Scotland and expense for England, Henry VIII had won no political advantage. On the contrary, the war had encouraged many neutrals in Scotland to turn against England; if anything, the English marriage was more unpopular in 1546 than it had been in 1543. Furthermore, Marie de Guise, who had come to take a more active role in politics, was using her influence in favour of a stronger French alliance. Her father and brothers were powerful men at the French court, and partly through their influence the French king sent over money and men in 1545 to help the Scots hold out against England, help that, though small-scale, greatly boosted Scottish morale. Notwithstanding French involvement in the war against England, there were no definite plans as yet for the Queen of Scots to marry a French prince, possibly because Arran harboured hopes that she might wed his own son.

Henry VIII's death on 28 January 1547 brought the nine-year-old Edward VI to the throne. His maternal uncle, the Earl of Hertford, newly created Duke of Somerset, was appointed Lord Protector of the realm and effectively controlled English policy until his fall from power in October 1549. During his period of rule, he pursued an all-out policy of aggression towards Scotland. Like Henry VIII, Somerset continued the 'Rough Wooing', seeking to impose by force a political union with England through the marriage of Edward to Mary. Additionally, however, he aimed at encouraging the Scots to espouse the religion of Protestantism, which so far had won only a minority of converts amongst the lairds. But despite the energy he was to bring to his campaign, an important change in the government of France ensured that it would fail. On 31 March 1547 François I died, to be succeeded by his ambitious, warlike son, Henri II. Henri's confidants included the two brothers of Marie de Guise – François, Duke of Aumale, and Charles, Cardinal of Guise – who easily persuaded the king to pursue an imperialist policy in Scotland. The Anglo-French conflict that ensued had a momentous effect on Mary Queen of Scots, resulting in her starting a new life in France.

Henri acted first, and, to the surprise of the English, in July 1547 sent an expedition to help Governor Arran capture St Andrew's Castle in Fife, which was then being held by a group of Protestants who had murdered Cardinal Beaton the previous year. Somerset responded by sending a force of about 15,000 men into the Eastern March of Scotland, which he intended to occupy and garrison. On 10 September the English troops arrived above the village of Pinkie, nine miles east of Edinburgh, where they met an unexpectedly large army raised by Arran; 23,000 men

strong, it was one of the largest Scottish forces ever mustered. But in the ensuing battle some 10,000 Scots were slaughtered, and a further fifteen hundred taken prisoner, leaving Somerset the victor and the way open to Edinburgh and Stirling. For fear of capture, Mary was conveyed hurriedly by night to the isolated Inchmahome Priory, situated on an island in the Lake of Menteith in the highlands of Perthshire, popularly known as 'The Trossachs'. There she stayed for three weeks with four young girls of about her own age before returning to Stirling, which Somerset had in fact made no attempt to seize. The duke was too preoccupied with constructing fortresses in the south-east that would give him military control over the area.

Arran, meanwhile, was making his own plans. Refusing to submit to Somerset, in January 1548 he made an agreement with Henri II that was intended to save Scotland from the English and reward his family. In return for French military aid, Mary was to be betrothed to the dauphin (the king's son and heir) and transported to France, where she would be raised in the royal household. Arran's own son was promised a French bride, and he himself would be granted the Duchy of Châtelherault in Poitou. Marie de Guise was apparently delighted with this deal, and helped Arran sell it to the Scottish nobility. Once they had given their consent in late February 1548, Mary was taken to Dumbarton Castle, on the west coast of Scotland, in readiness for her voyage to France. There she fell seriously ill, either from

The Rough Wooing

OPPOSITE

The 'Rough Wooing' letter, written by the commanders of the English army in Scotland (the Earl of Hertford, Lord Lisle and Sir Ralph Sadler) to Henry VIII on 18 May 1544. They describe the last phase of their raid into the Lowlands to punish the Scots for rejecting the marriage treaty between Mary and Edward. In their previous letter to Henry they had written of their determination to depart homewards with the army 'upon Thursday last' and to devastate the country 'as we might conveniently' on their way. They now triumphantly report, 'So have we now accomplished the same'.

Before departing Leith, they burnt Edinburgh and 'sondry other towns and villages' and 'we did

likewise burn the town of Legh [Leith], the same morning that we departed there', and either burnt or conveyed away 'such ships and boats as we found in the haven'. The writers continue with listing the other places and main houses burnt by the army on its way south. Ten lines from the bottom they report that the Scots failed to offer any effective resistance:

'And yesterday, the Lords Hume and Seton, and also as we were informed the earl Bothwell had assembled hither the number of 2,000 horsemen and 6,000 footmen, and were once determined to have stopped us at the [river] Peese, which is a very strait and ill passage for an army.'

Three thousand men 'being men of heart and having captains of any policy and experience of the wars' should have been able to keep the ford against a superior force, but the Scots dispersed when they saw the English army march towards them. (British Library, Additional MS 32654, f. 198)

LEFT

An Epistle or Exhortacion to Unitie and Peace, London, 1548. After the Duke of Somerset defeated the Scots at Pinkie, he tried to persuade them to agree to the marriage of Mary to Edward VI. The epistle, a piece of English propaganda, was addressed to the people of Scotland and tried to persuade them of the justice of the English cause and the benefits of a union with England. It circulated lowland Scotland during February 1548. (British Library, G5912 T/P)

Please it your Grace to understand that like as we wrote
in our last sent to your Mate our determynacion to depart from
Leith homeward, by cause of your & armye suppon finisshing
fast, and so to defeace the countrey by the waye in our
retourne as we might conveniently, So sone we noysse
accomplisshed the same, & we haiff before our departure
from Leith, geving brent Edenburgh and sondrye other
townes and villages in those partes as we wrote in our
forsaid last sent, we did likewise brent the towne of Leith
the same mornyng that we depted thens, and suche shippes
and botte as we founde in the haven mete to the brunyng of
moneye, we haue conveyd thens by see, and the rest
were brent, and also some distroyed and brent the pyere
of the haven, whereby Damayne, we thinke they shall
not be able to entollch a yoynght in our tyme, And in our
waye homeward, we haue brent the towne of
Muskelburgh, prestton, seton as the Lorde Setons
principall house, hym self being present & a loos from
us as a restren number of horsemen, as he might wall
see his owne house and the towne on fyere, And also
we haue brent the townes of Cardington and Donbarr
where we were assured your Mate he will brent, with
as many other pretie gentlemens and other houses and
villages, where we might conveniently ordre this
the brynage as composs of our waye homeward, And
allwayes had fynge respect to the keping of good ordre and
arraye in our marchyng, as notwithstandyng the Erolle
were dayly perinte about us and make so many grounde
fences and brayge, they coulde take us at none advantage
And yesterday the Lorde Home and Seton, and also
as we were enfermed Erolle Bothwell had assembled
hither the number of as of horsemen and as in fote
men, and were one determyned to some stopped us at the
passe, where is a narow straict and ill passage for an
armye, & thynkyng your Mate that as as as men, being
men of haist and haveing Capertaynes of any pollusie
or experyence of the warres, might defend and kepe the
said passage ayaynst a gretter power than we had,
Me dowtelesse beyng the said Erolle, assembled and

smallpox or more likely measles, but she had
recovered her health by the time that French
galleys arrived at Dumbarton at the end of July
to convey her to France.

The royal convoy embarked on 29 July 1548
but had to wait until the wind allowed them
to sail on 7 August. Amongst those
accompanying the young queen were her
newly appointed guardians, Lords Erskine and
Livingston, several ladies, most notably her
half-sister Lady Janet Fleming (an illegitimate
daughter of James V), her nurse Jean Sinclair,
and the four noble girls about her own age
who had previously gone with her to
Inchmahome. They were nicknamed the four
Maries: Mary Fleming, Mary Beaton, Mary
Livingston and Mary Seton. Also on board
the ship were three of her illegitimate half-
brothers, including the eldest, the seventeen-
year-old James Stewart, who was then making
a short visit to France. Marie de Guise, though,
stayed behind in Scotland to watch over her
daughter's interests. Although the parting
from her mother was tearful, Mary seemed to
be excited by the voyage and clearly enjoyed
the fact that she was less seasick than any one
of her party; indeed, wrote her French escort,
the Sieur de Brézé, 'she made fun of those
who were'.[4]

The route taken was long and hazardous,
chosen to avoid interception from English
ships. After eight days the ship landed close
to Roscoff in Brittany on 15 August, and from
there Mary was conducted in short stages to
the Château de Carrières-sur-Seine, west of

Paris, where Henri's children were based.
En route some of the men were taken ill with
stomach problems, while the young brother
of Mary Seton died of a similar complaint,
but Mary herself remained well and cheerful.
During her journey she entered the important
towns of Nantes and Angers in spectacular
processions designed to present her to
observers as both a monarch in her own right
and Henri's own daughter.

Once at Carrières, most of her Scottish
attendants were ordered to return home,
and the four Maries were packed off to a
Dominican convent school. This separation
came about in part because Henri wanted the
young queen to be served only by French
people so that she could learn the language
and manners of her new home. Furthermore,
the French court was one of the most
sophisticated in Europe, and Mary's own
countrymen and women were thought to be
unattractive, unrefined and ill-washed, and,
as such, unsuitable companions for the
prospective wife of the dauphin.

Henri decided that Mary was to be brought up
in the royal household alongside his legitimate
children, and treated as if she were his own
daughter. By then, he and his wife, Catherine
de' Medici, had produced four children: the
dauphin François, born on 19 January 1544,
Elizabeth, who was a year younger, the toddler
Claude, and the newly born Louis, who was to
die of measles in 1550. Between 1550 and 1554,
four more children arrived in the royal
nursery, two of whom – Charles and Henri –

later succeeded as kings of France. As a crowned monarch and the bride-to-be of the heir to the French throne, Mary was given precedence over all the royal children except François. In the royal palaces she shared the best apartments with Elizabeth, who soon became her closest friend.

Mary seems to have been an enchanting child. Very pretty, graceful and regal, she made an excellent impression on the new people she met. Her grandmother, Antoinette de Guise, praised her looks: 'her complexion is fine and clear, and her skin white. The lower part of her face is very well formed, the eyes are small and rather deep-set, the face is rather long. She is graceful and self-assured'.[5] According to the Sieur de Brézé, 'the king thinks her the prettiest and most graceful little princess he has ever seen', while a certain Monsieur de Lorges wrote to Marie de Guise in a similar vein: Mary was so 'amiable and intelligent' that everyone was delighted with her.[6] All reports claimed that the young dauphin was very fond of the young queen and that the king mightily enjoyed her company.

The first court festivity Mary attended was the wedding in December 1548 of her uncle François to Anne d'Este, daughter of the Duke of Ferrara. During the dancing Henri II took the opportunity to parade Mary before the English ambassador, who was forced to grit his teeth and say nothing. Over the next ten years Mary was to enjoy many more balls and entertainments. To ensure she was suitably attired for such occasions, she was provided with a lavish wardrobe. Her accounts of 1551 reveal that her dresses were made from crimson Venetian satin, gold damask on crimson silk, and rich black taffeta, while her caps were elaborately embroidered and her gloves made of the finest leather. At that time she possessed at least ten pairs of shoes in a variety of colours – white, black, purple, red and yellow – while her jewels were so numerous that three brass chests could barely contain them. Amongst them were a golden chain set with pearls and green enamel, and a gold ring with a ruby in it. Even these were not thought sufficient for her rank on certain state occasions, for in February 1553 her uncle, the cardinal, suggested to Marie de Guise that he should lend Mary some jewels belonging to their sister.

Despite Henri's wish to separate Mary from her Scottish companions, Marie de Guise insisted that Lady Janet Fleming continue as her governess and Jean Sinclair as her nurse. Both women, however, came under the direction of Jean de Humières, who, until his death in July 1550, directed the children's household with the help of his wife. Then Claude d'Urfé took over until 1553, assisted by Madame de Humières. Mademoiselle de Curel taught the child French and 'the accomplishments which will be wanted here'; other tutors included Claude Millot and Antoine Fouquelin. In addition to French, Mary learnt Spanish and Italian, which apparently 'she employed more for use than for show or lively talk', and Latin which she understood better than she could speak.[7]

Clearly, unlike her English cousin, Princess Elizabeth Tudor, Mary had no great talent for languages and, indeed, was no scholar. She did, however, have a love of poetry. In her library were works of Ovid and Virgil, and for enjoyment she read those of the contemporary French poets Pierre de Ronsard and Joachim du Bellay, which were said to move her to tears. She later attempted to compose her own sonnets in French and Italian; the first was written when she was seventeen on the pages of her Mass book.

Mary was also very fond of music. She learnt to play the lute, cittern, harp and harpsichord, and was described as having a very sweet and true singing voice. She also danced excellently, showing herself to be agile and graceful. Another skill she acquired and enjoyed was embroidery: aged nine, she began her training under the supervision of the king's personal embroiderer, beginning with knitting and sewing, and progressing to elaborate and fine stitches. As for outdoor sports, Mary liked a game of tennis, but adored riding and hunting. For these pursuits, she began her training on a pony, and then came to adopt the French practice of riding astride the horse rather than side-saddle. Both Henri's influential mistress, Diane de Poitiers, and his wife Catherine took a close interest in the rearing of the royal children. Members of the Guise family also watched over Mary and reported her progress to Marie de Guise, who continued to supervise her daughter's upbringing and write to her regularly from Scotland.

ABOVE

Portrait of Anne d'Este, after 1566 by François Clouet. Anne was the daughter of the Duke of Ferrara and the wife of Mary's uncle, François, 2nd Duke of Guise. Their wedding, on 4 December 1548, was the first public event Mary attended in France. Mary became very close to her aunt, who helped supervise her education. This portrait was drawn around the time of Anne's marriage in 1566 to her second husband, the Duke of Nemours. (Musée Condé, Chantilly)

OPPOSITE

Portrait of Dauphin François, 1552 by Jean Clouet. The inscription states that this portrait of the eldest son of Henri II and Catherine de' Medici was drawn in July 1552, when the dauphin was aged eight years and five months. Six years later he married Mary, and in July 1559 he became King of France, but died the following December. (Musée Condé, Chantilly)

Françoys daulphin de France en l'age
de huict ans et cinq mois au mois de
Juillet l'an 1552

In 1550 Marie arranged a trip to France to be reunited with her family. It had been two years since she had last seen her daughter, and twelve since she had been separated from her son and parents. Before her departure, however, Marie's father died, leaving her eldest brother François as the Duke of Guise and head of the family. The death of her uncle John, Cardinal of Lorraine, occurred shortly afterwards, and resulted in the promotion of her brother Charles (the Cardinal of Guise) to the more prestigious see of Lorraine. Marie missed both funerals, as she had to remain in Scotland to oversee the cessation of hostilities between England and France. The war in Scotland had gone badly for England, and Edward VI's government was forced during 1550 to withdraw its troops and dismantle its garrisons in the south-east of the northern realm. At last, in the late summer of 1550, Marie was free to leave for France, and on 19 September she landed with a large retinue of Scots at Dieppe in Normandy.

Awaiting Marie at Dieppe were the new Duke of Guise and the Duke of Longueville, her fifteen-year-old son by her first marriage. Seven-year-old Mary, who had just recovered from dysentery, remained with the royal family at Rouen, and it was there that she was publicly reunited with her mother on 5 September. Six days later, on 1 October, Henri II staged a triumphal royal entry into the Norman capital, an event that was designed to honour Marie for her management of Scotland and to celebrate his recent military successes against the English.

Even by the standards of the French court, the ceremonial was spectacular. In a colourful victory parade, replicas of forts captured from the English in France were displayed on poles; marching before French soldiers were English prisoners of war; and men dressed up as Roman soldiers carried banners painted with those sites successfully defended or captured by the French in Scotland. Even more splendid were the floats that followed; elaborately decorated, they symbolized Henri's eternal fame as a victor in war, and signalled his global ambitions to be the ruler of a powerful French empire. To drive home the message that this Renaissance pageant was at least in part a visual representation of Mary's role in French dynastic politics, the Scottish queen rode alongside the dauphin just behind a chariot on which a winged Fortune held an imperial crown over the head of a laurelled warrior who represented the French king.

Marie de Guise stayed in France for just over a year. During the winter she and her Scottish entourage resided at Blois as the honoured guests of the king. There discussions were held about the future government of Scotland, and it was agreed that Marie would have to return to Edinburgh to protect her daughter's interests and advance those of the French. But Marie was in no hurry to leave her children, and in the spring of 1551 she joined the royal progress in northern France, travelling with the court to Tours, Angers and Nantes, before setting off to visit her family at Joinville. The tour was somewhat blighted, however, when in April 1551 news broke of an assassination plot

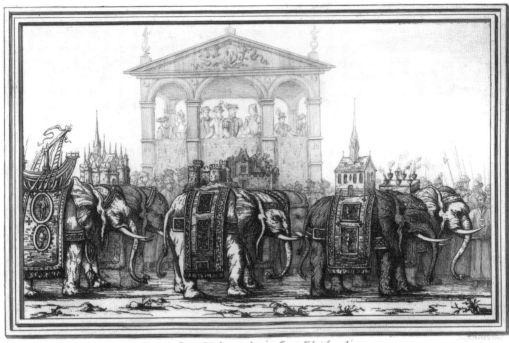

Templa focos Vrbes palatia Sex Elephanti
Cæfatas naues victaq, Caftra gerunt,

to murder the young Mary. An archer in Henri's Scottish guard had suborned the cook to poison her favourite dish of frittered pears. Luckily the plot was uncovered in time and Mary escaped unharmed. Her mother, however, was so distressed by the incident that she became quite ill. Five months later she had to face a real tragedy, for just before her departure to Scotland her son suddenly sickened and died in her arms. Marie was heartbroken, but stayed only for the burial, which Mary did not attend. Marie set sail to Scotland in October 1551, never to see her one surviving child again.

Despite missing her mother, Mary flourished in France. In December 1551 the Constable of

Marie de Guise's visit to France and Henri II's entry into Rouen in October 1550. This 1866 engraving by L. de Merval shows Henri's triumphal entry into Rouen, where Mary was to meet her mother, Marie de Guise. Amongst the floats were papier mâché elephants, which symbolized military power and prowess, and were propelled forward by men inside. These elephants followed bands of military men. On their backs were models of forts in France won from the English. (British Library, AC 8938/18)

France, Anne de Montmorency (a man, despite his name), wrote that she had grown 'in grace and virtue',[8] and early the following year, her aunt Anne d'Este reported that Mary could no longer be treated as a child, as her conversation and deportment were too mature. Every day, it was said, she grew 'more suited' to become the bride of a future king of France.[9] Her education was becoming more advanced, as suited her years and position. She was introduced to Plutarch, Plautus and Cicero in Latin, and completed her own Latin compositions and translations. Other works she read included the colloquies of Erasmus and extracts translated into French from Plato's *Republic*. Although she actually owned the complete works of Plato in Greek, it is unlikely that she was sufficiently fluent in that language to be able to read and understand the texts. Around May 1555, when she was nearly thirteen, Mary delivered an oration in Latin before the king and queen, her uncles and other members of the court in the Great Hall of the Louvre. Not a natural Latin speaker, Mary prepared well for the occasion. Not only did she choose a subject that she had written about in some fifteen previous exercises, but she also borrowed liberally from a published work by the writer François Dubois. Appropriately, her speech argued that an education in letters and the liberal arts was suitable for women.

Although educated as a French princess, Mary was not allowed to forget the Scottish language, and on occasion, probably to impress or amuse the French court, she dressed up in Scottish national dress. As she grew older, she was kept informed about current events in Scotland by her mother. The Cardinal of Lorraine, meanwhile, taught her to be a political animal, and especially to keep her affairs secret. Accordingly she kept her correspondence under lock and key and directed her private secretary to put politically sensitive passages of her letters in cipher. Despite this caution, Mary trusted her mother implicitly and would sign blank sheets for Marie to use for official purposes in the administration of Scotland.

In 1551 changes were made to Mary's household. After giving birth to Henri II's bastard, Lady Janet Fleming was dismissed in disgrace and in her place was appointed Françoise d'Estampville, Madame de Parois, whom Mary did not find anything like as congenial. At about the same time the Cardinal of Lorraine started to supervise Mary's upbringing more closely. Every month he examined her household in order, he said, 'to find out in detail all that is going on'.[10] As his political ambitions depended heavily on his niece's marriage to the dauphin, he was determined to ensure that her reputation and status were properly maintained, especially now that she was growing into womanhood. The appointment of the conventional and

OPPOSITE
Portrait of Cardinal Charles of Lorraine, c.1550 by François Clouet. The cardinal, Mary's uncle, was largely responsible for the supervision of her education and household in France. His elder brother was François, 2nd Duke of Guise.
(Musée Condé, Chantilly)

pious Madame de Parois took care of her reputation, but problems remained for several years about the size of her household and the money available for her personal expenditure, both of which touched her outward status. In truth, Mary's household soon became short-staffed. In 1553 Madame de Curel resigned after a quarrel with Parois, while other servants were leaving to marry or drifting away to take up other posts that were better and more regularly paid. Soon afterwards Parois complained that she and Jean Sinclair were Mary's only female attendants and that she was forced to dress Mary's hair in the absence of other women.

Just four days after Mary turned eleven, Henri II informed the Governor of Scotland – Arran, who was now the Duke of Châtelherault – that Mary had come of age and chosen her mother to be her 'curator' or regent. Henri had pretty much decided upon this change of regime while Marie de Guise was in France, but had been forced to wait until Mary had reached her majority before he could initiate the transfer of power. In December 1553, however, he could afford to delay no longer, as he feared that Châtelherault was about to abandon the French alliance and was intriguing with the new English queen, Mary I. Consequently, even though Scottish tradition dictated that a girl reached her majority only after she had completed her twelfth year, at Henri's prompting the Parlement of Paris judged that Mary could take control of her kingdom at any time during her twelfth year – that is, while she was only eleven years old.

Two weeks after this judgment, Mary was established in her own separate household. On 1 January 1554 she marked the occasion of her new independent status by inviting her uncle, the Cardinal of Lorraine, to dine with her. According to Parois, Mary was delighted to be mistress of her own establishment and enjoyed issuing orders to her servants. But the new regime did not end earlier problems. Although new servants were hired, Mary's household continued to be understaffed, mainly because of a shortage of funds. Brought in to review the situation in 1555, when Parois was sick, Antoinette de Guise was shocked to see her granddaughter with so few attendants; Mary, she reported, was forced to sleep with only a waiting woman, which was totally unsuitable for a young lady.

The money was also not available to keep Mary in the style she desired. On one occasion in 1554 she begged for some new fashionable dresses; on another she implored for embroidered 'ciphers' (probably her initials) to be sewn on to her dresses as was then the vogue at court. She likewise asked Parois to plead with her mother for a gown of cloth of gold to wear at a particular court wedding, complaining that the French princesses had been given cloth-of-gold and cloth-of-silver gowns for the marriage, yet she had nothing. Concerned at the mounting household expenses, the cardinal suggested economies, but Mary refused point blank to accept any recommendations that would result in her being detached from the main body of the court during its customary peregrinations.

Portrait of Antoinette de Guise. Mary's maternal grandmother was born Antoinette de Bourbon, and married the Duke of Guise in 1515. A strong and forceful character, she helped supervise Mary while she was in France. (Bibliothèque Nationale, Paris)

Why Mary's household was so short of money is not entirely clear. Accusations were made that cash had been pocketed or misappropriated by her officers, but while there certainly appears to have been some mismanagement, it is also true that Marie de Guise simply could not afford to pay out the huge sums it cost to keep her daughter in the style of a French princess. As Henri refused to make any contribution, the whole amount had to be financed out of Marie's French pension, her dowry from the Longueville estates and the Scottish treasury.

To make matters worse, Mary fell out with Madame de Parois. Increasingly, the young queen resented her governess's tutelage, especially when Parois interfered with her running of the household. Arguments arose whenever Mary wanted to raise the servants' wages or to give away her old gowns and other possessions. In Mary's opinion, Parois was making her look mean by objecting to her generosity, and she also became distressed when her governess told tales about her to her mother, grandmother and to Catherine de' Medici. At the end of 1555 the two had a serious row. Mary had given away some dresses that she had outgrown to her Guise aunts, who were abbesses and would use the rich material from the garments as altar cloths. But Parois disrespectfully challenged her decision and claimed the items for herself. After this quarrel, Parois left Mary's household to go to Paris, and sometime in 1557 she resigned or was dismissed. From then on Mary's household was supervised by her

grandmother and her aunt, Anne d'Este, from their respective homes.

Mary complained that the quarrel with Parois had made her ill, but generally her health was good during her time in France. She had episodic fainting fits and indigestion, which doctors blamed on excessive eating, but only two serious illnesses. One was smallpox, which she incurred at some unknown date, but, thanks to the treatment of the king's physician, it left her unmarked. The second serious bout of sickness afflicted her in August 1556, when with other members of the court she went down with a high fever, a form of malaria, known as the 'sweat' or 'quartan' ague. During its critical phase, Queen Catherine 'hardly ever' left her night or day,[11] and even after the worst was over, Catherine stayed by her bedside. The importance of Mary in French dynastic politics was again evident.

In the autumn of 1557 Henri decided the time was right for Mary's marriage to his son. At the end of October he informed the Scottish parliament that the wedding would be celebrated in early 1558 immediately after his son's fourteenth birthday, the minimum age for marriage. Eight Scottish commissioners, including Mary's eldest half-brother Lord James Stewart, consequently arrived in France in February to negotiate the matrimonial treaty. Following the instructions of the Scottish parliament, they insisted that the country's independence should be preserved. Mary and François therefore pledged to observe the laws, liberties and privileges of

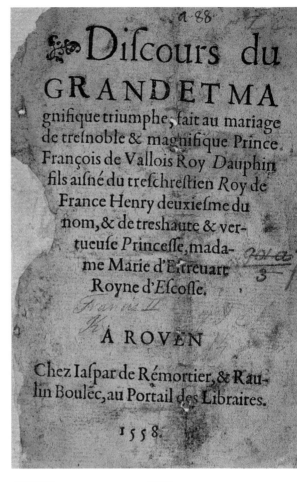

OPPOSITE

Portrait of Mary Aged about Sixteen, c.1558 by François Clouet. Painted shortly before her marriage, this portrait depicts a modest, innocent but regal young woman.
(Bibliothèque Nationale, Paris)

ABOVE

The frontispiece of *Discours du grand et magnifique triumphe fait au mariage de tresnoble [et] magnifique Prince François de Vallois ... [et] de treshaute [et] vertueuse Princesse madame Marie d'Estruart Royne d'Escosse* (1558). This pamphlet described the wedding of Mary and François at the Cathedral of Notre-Dame in Paris on 24 April 1558. Public interest was great.
(British Library, 905.a.15)

Scotland, expressly adding that should Mary die without issue, her nearest blood relative, namely James Hamilton, Duke of Châtelherault, would inherit her throne. But Scotland's independence did not fit in with Henri II's plans. As a result, despite these assurances, three secret documents were signed by Mary on 4 April 1558 that completely nullified the agreed arrangements. In them, failing heirs from her marriage, she bequeathed her realm to the King of France, assigned to him full rights to the revenues of Scotland as compensation for sums spent on her education in France and its defence against England, and annulled any promises that she might make to the contrary. Mary was thus implicated in an act of deliberate deception against the Scots, led to do so by her family in France. Whether or not she had actually read the three documents is debatable; as already mentioned, on several occasions previously she had signed blank sheets for her mother's use.

The betrothal of the young couple took place on 19 April 1558 in the Great Hall of the Louvre, their hands ceremoniously and appropriately joined together by the Cardinal of Lorraine. At the ball to celebrate the occasion Mary and Henri II led the dancing. Five days after their betrothal, on the second Sunday after Easter, Mary and the dauphin were married at Notre-Dame in Paris. The wedding was a magnificent and widely publicized event, for it was the first time a dauphin had been married in Paris for over two hundred years. The long wedding procession led by Mary's uncle François, the

Duke of Guise, set off in the morning from the nearby episcopal palace, and was viewed by a large crowd. The fifteen-year-old Mary looked magnificent: her white dress was covered with jewels and decorated with white embroidery, while her long train of grey velvet was held by two young girls. From her neck hung a sparkling jewelled pendant, a gift from her father-in-law, and on her head sat a specially commissioned gold crown studded with precious rubies, sapphires and pearls, the huge stone in the centre rumoured to have cost the enormous sum of over half a million crowns. What the bridegroom wore was not reported, but the short and puny François must have looked considerably less impressive than his tall and attractive bride. At the west door of the church, in an open pavilion twelve feet high, the Cardinal of Bourbon performed the nuptial rite of putting the ring on the bride, and the Bishop of Paris gave an address. Then they all moved inside for the celebration of Mass by the bishop.

The religious ceremony was immediately followed by a sumptuous wedding banquet in the episcopal palace. During the feast Mary's head ached from wearing the heavy crown, so Henri ordered the lord-in-waiting to hold it over her throughout the meal. Around five o'clock the royal party again showed itself to the Parisian crowd as it made its way by a circuitous route to the Palais de Justice for the evening's revelries, Mary sitting with Queen Catherine in a golden litter and the dauphin following alongside his father on horseback. The evening's revelries included supper, dancing, mummeries, masques and other pastimes. Organized by the Duke of Guise, they were described by the Venetian Giovanni Michiel as 'the most regal and triumphant' witnessed at the French court for many years.[12] The masques were especially sophisticated, employing elaborate floats on mechanical devices to create a stunning effect. The fête continued the following day at the Louvre, and culminated in a three-day tournament at Tournelles, Henri II's favourite palace in Paris. It is unsurprising that so much money was lavished on this wedding, given that the dynastic marriage marked the high point of both Henri II's ambitions to absorb Scotland into France and the Guise family's aspirations to put itself at the centre of power at the French court. Mary was very excited by the event; we cannot know if she loved her new husband, but on the morning of her wedding day she described herself as 'one of the happiest women in the world'.[13]

Although Mary's marriage had long been an integral part of Henri II's foreign policy, its actual timing probably owed much to the immediate international situation. Since April 1557 Henri had been at war with Queen Mary of England and her Habsburg husband, Philip of Spain, and although Scotland was technically his ally, Marie de Guise had struggled to provide Henri with military assistance. According to Giacomo Soranzo, the Venetian ambassador in Paris, one of Henri's aims in 'hastening this marriage'[14] was to tighten French control over Scotland so that Marie de Guise would find it easier to raise an army against England during the next campaigning season. The capture of Calais in January 1558 obviated this need, but the marriage then became desirable as a reward for the Duke of Guise who had led the successful campaign. Additionally, Henri may also have decided to proceed with the marriage at that time in order to advance his imperial ambitions. As Mary I of England was then forty-one years old and still childless, Mary Stewart could be promoted as her successor in preference to her half-sister Elizabeth Tudor, whom Catholics believed was illegitimate.

Mary's marriage to the dauphin fulfilled the hopes of all her family. Like most other royals in the sixteenth century, she was the pawn of dynastic politics. Yet Mary was content with this fate. Even though her husband was unprepossessing and immature, she had grown fond of him as a child and found him affectionate and attentive. Moreover, the playful life of a princess satisfied her greatly, as she delighted in dancing, riding, falconry and hunting. She showed no interest in taking on political responsibilities, and no sign of frustration at her powerlessness or the continual interference of her family. Pliable, eager to please and essentially passive, Mary Queen of Scots had not yet shown any capacity to rule, or even to make independent political decisions. Only in the personal sphere – in her fight with Parois – did Mary display an independent streak and some strength of character, yet even here it is significant that her attempts to be self-assertive caused her such stress that she fell ill.

Queen-Dauphine and Queen of France 1558–1560

AFTER HER MARRIAGE in 1558 Mary was known in France as the 'queen-dauphine', while François was called the 'king-dauphin'. In Scotland they were styled as king and queen, and in November 1558 the Scottish parliament granted François the crown matrimonial, which meant that he assumed all of Mary's rights and powers as sovereign. Concerned to safeguard his own position as heir presumptive, the Duke of Châtelherault publicly protested at the parliamentary move, and used his influence to prevent the dispatch of the crown to France. The remaining Scottish lords, however, seemed generally unthreatened by the Franco-Scottish dynastic union, for in practical terms no significant alteration took place in the government of the realm. Marie de Guise continued as regent, although state documents were now signed by Mary and François jointly. Unsurprisingly in a patriarchal age, the signature of François was always given precedence by appearing on the left-hand side, where it would be read first.

Despite their youth and François's physical immaturity, it seems likely that the marriage was immediately consummated. The Venetian ambassador reported as such, and Mary believed herself to be pregnant, first in August 1559 and then again in the summer of 1560. The couple shared the same lodgings although, as was normal, they each had their own bedroom. Otherwise, not much changed for the queen-dauphine, and she participated in the usual round of parties, weddings and feasts. Towards the end of 1558, however, she was suddenly at the centre of a political storm. On 17 November Mary I of England died, leaving no children. Her half-sister, Elizabeth Tudor, was immediately proclaimed the new queen and crowned in January 1559. Elizabeth's legitimacy, however, was contested by some Catholics, for the pope had refused to annul Henry VIII's first marriage to Katherine of Aragon and to recognize his second to Elizabeth's mother, Anne Boleyn. Furthermore, Elizabeth was a Protestant, and it became evident in early 1559 that she intended to break the ties Mary I had restored with Rome and to reintroduce a Protestant form of worship to England. On the grounds of both Elizabeth's illegitimacy and her religion, Henri II decided to promote his daughter-in-law as the rightful queen of England and pursue his imperial ambition to extend French power throughout the British Isles.

Mary's claim to the English throne came through her grandmother Margaret Tudor, the elder daughter of Henry VII, who had married James IV of Scotland. For those Catholics who did not recognize the validity of Henry VIII's second marriage, Mary was the nearest in blood to both Henrys, and therefore had the best hereditary right to the English throne in 1558. Elizabeth's title, however, was upheld by parliamentary statute, since the 1544 Act of Succession had named her next in line to Mary Tudor, and on that basis most English Catholics were prepared to accept Elizabeth's accession. Nonetheless, it obviously suited the French king and Guise family to dispute Elizabeth's title. As early as December 1558, Henri's agents in Rome were working on the pope to come out in support of the Scottish queen; in fact, the pope refused to do this because of the offence it would cause to Philip II of Spain, who was determined that England should not come under French control.

OPPOSITE

Engraving of Mary Aged Seventeen, 1559 by an unknown artist. This engraving was published in Antwerp, probably just after Mary became Queen of France. It was not made from life, but was based on contemporary coins that showed her head in profile.
(British Museum)

Margarite dangleterre D'vgne leftura feur deHenry vng
D vg dangleterre femme de Jacques III Roy d'escosse

Mary's Claim to the English Throne

Portrait of Margaret Tudor, *c.*1503 by an unknown artist. Margaret, Mary's paternal grandmother, was the elder daughter of Henry VII, and in August 1503 married James IV of Scotland. This sketch was probably made about the time of her wedding, which was celebrated in poetry as the union of the thistle and the rose, for she holds a rose in her hand. It was through Margaret that Mary laid claim to the English throne.
(British Museum)

The arms of Marie quene dolphines of france
The nobillest ladie jn earth, for till advance
Of Scotland quene And of jnglond also
Of Ireland als God hath providit so

The coat of arms displayed by Mary when Queen-dauphine of France. The English ambassador in France sent this drawing back to the Privy Council as evidence that Mary and her husband were quartering their arms with those of England, and thereby laying a claim to the throne of England. The verses in translation read:

The arms of Marie queen dauphine of France
The noblest lady in earth for till advance:
Of Scotland Queen and of England also
Of Ireland also God hath provided so.

(British Library, Cotton Caligula B X, f. 18)

Just as provocatively, in January 1559, Mary and her husband began to style themselves as 'King and Queen Dauphins of Scotland, England and Ireland', and to quarter their arms with those of England. Furthermore, during negotiations to bring the war between France and England to a close, Henri II raised the issue of Mary's title, using it as an excuse for not restoring Calais to Elizabeth.

Henri, however, could not afford to use military force on behalf of Mary's claim as he needed an international peace, at least in the short term, for financial reasons. Consequently, he let Mary's claims slip away in return for a treaty signed at Cateau-Cambrésis, which bound France, Scotland and England to remain in amity for at least eight years. By its terms the French were to retain Calais for those eight years and then either return it to England or else pay an indemnity in lieu. On 18 April 1559 Mary and François ratified the treaty, and on 28 May Mary told the English commissioners that she was content with the newly concluded peace with England and would do everything in her power to preserve it. She had more cause to do so, she said, 'for that your Majestie [Elizabeth] was her cousin and good sister'.[15]

Yet even after peace was agreed, Mary continued to display the arms of England, while Constable Anne de Montmorency, no friend to the Guises, claimed in June 1559 that the queen-dauphine had 'right and title to England'.[16] Understandably, this behaviour and these utterances greatly alarmed the English government, especially when the College of Heralds in England warned Elizabeth that the arms borne by Mary were 'prejudicial to the Queen, her state and dignity'.[17] The only bright light for the English in this difficult political situation was that Mary had fallen sick and seemed not long for this world. In the spring of 1559 the English ambassador Sir John Mason reported home: 'The Queen of Scots is very sick, and these men fear she will not long continue,' adding 'God take her to Him so soon as may please Him.' When the new English ambassador Sir Nicholas Throckmorton was taken to meet Mary towards the end of May, he found her looking extremely ill, 'very pale and green, and withal short breathed and it is whispered here among them that she cannot long live'.[18] In mid-June, while at church, Mary had a fainting spell and was given wine from the altar to stop her passing out. Throckmorton wrote that he had never before seen her look so ill, and repeated opinions that she would not live long. But Mary did not die. Indeed, she outlived her father-in-law, who was wounded in a jousting accident on 30 June 1559 and expired ten days afterwards. Suddenly and unexpectedly, Mary became queen consort of France at sixteen years old.

Immediately upon her husband's accession, Mary set off for the royal apartments at Saint-Germain, and one of her earliest actions was to direct the late king's long-standing mistress Diane de Poitiers to draw up an inventory of her jewels so that she could take over all those that had been gifts from Henri II.

Letter from Mary and her husband François to Queen Elizabeth, dated 21 April 1559. They express pleasure at the peace of Cateau-Cambrésis, which had just been concluded between England and France. They explain that they have sent their ratification of the treaty to England by Maitland of Lethington, and ask permission that he might take it to Marie de Guise in Scotland. Mary used her usual signature 'Marie', and it follows that of François.
(British Library, Cotton Caligula B X, f. 8)

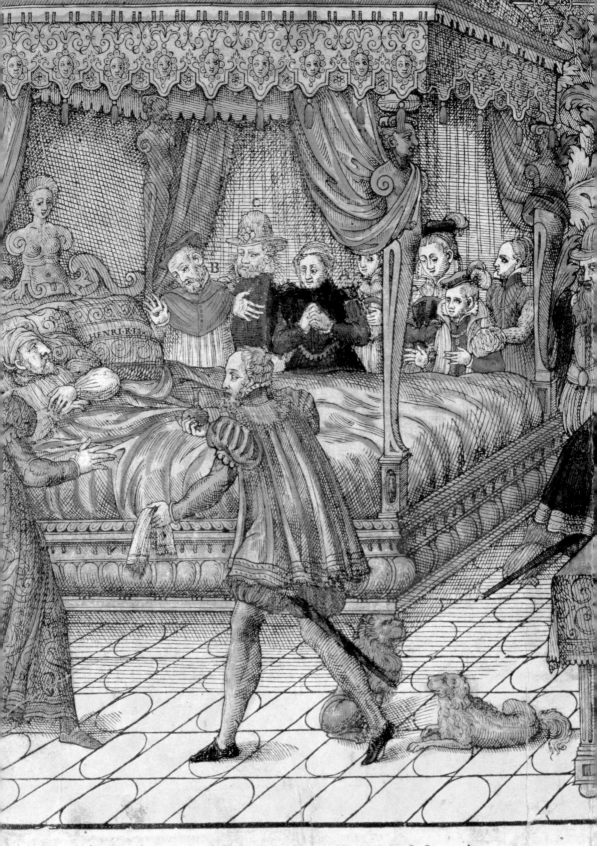

A· La Royne pleurant.
B. Le Cardinal de Lorraine.
C. M. le Connestable.
D. Postes courans & des medecins & C

giens bien experts, enuoyés de Flandres par le
Roy d'Espaigne.
E. Gardes de la chambre du Roy.
F. Medecins & Cirurgiens.

François, meanwhile, went to the house of the Cardinal of Lorraine in Paris and then to a Guise chateau just outside the city. With the death of Henri II, the Guise family became the dominant force in political life. Until then, the Cardinal of Lorraine and Duke of Guise had been forced to share power with the Constable of France and his ally Diane de Poitiers. But as early as 11 July 1559 Throckmorton reported gloomily that 'the house of Guise is like to govern all about the King, who is much affected towards them', and two days later he pronounced: 'The House of Guise ruleth'.[19] He was right: the duke controlled the king's household and military affairs, while his brother, the cardinal, took control of the kingdom's administrative and financial affairs. The danger, from Throckmorton's point of view, was that the duke and cardinal would promote the pretensions of their niece to the English throne. Consequently, the ambassador waited anxiously to see what title the new king would use and what coat of arms would appear on his seal. To his relief, on the day of Henri II's funeral, 11 August 1559, François was

proclaimed solely as 'King of France', and the seal he used in France was entirely traditional. But on 9 September the ambassador learnt to his dismay that the new great seal to be used in Scotland bore the arms of England, France and Scotland quartered. Furthermore, when the king made his entry into Reims for the coronation, these arms were displayed very prominently over the main gate.

François's coronation had been planned for Sunday 17 September 1559, but it was postponed for a day because of the illness of an important participant. Hence François II was to be the first French king to be crowned neither on a Sunday nor a feast day. Naturally, Mary attended the ceremony, sitting alongside Catherine de' Medici and her daughters. But, unlike the other ladies of the royal party, who wore black out of respect for the dead king, Mary was dressed in the *deuil blanc* – white widow's weeds. Although white was the traditional royal colour of mourning, Mary's decision to set herself apart from the other members of the royal family was an early sign of independence that set tongues wagging.

During much of her husband's reign Mary continued to experience ill health. In August 1559 the Spanish ambassador told Throckmorton that she 'looked very evil; and was so weak' especially after meals; the next month she seemed a little better, but in October she again suffered from fainting fits. In November she 'kept her chamber all the day long'.[20] These attacks are usually diagnosed as stress related, since throughout her life Mary's

PREVIOUS PAGES

The Deathbed of Henri II of France, 1559 by Jacques Tortorel and Jean Perrisin. In this woodcut Mary can be seen in profile beside the bedpost on the right, and the much shorter dauphin stands beside her. The figure marked B is the Cardinal of Lorraine, and C is the Constable Anne de Montmorency. (Private collection/ Bridgeman Art Library) health tended to break down whenever she came under pressure, and during 1559 and 1560 she was unquestionably subject to personal and political anxieties. At the personal level, Mary was preparing during the summer of 1559 for separation from two of her closest companions – her husband's sisters Elizabeth and Claude – both of whom had recently married. Although Mary would be able to visit Claude in her relatively nearby new home in Lorraine, Elizabeth departed for Spain in November 1559 as the new wife of Philip II, and it seemed unlikely that the friends would meet again. During the same period, Mary was possibly experiencing strains in her relationship with Catherine de' Medici. On the death of her husband, Catherine was unwilling to slip into the background as queen dowager, but instead insisted on being called 'queen mother' and exercising political power in the interests of her son. Although there were no outward signs of tension between the two women, several contemporary writers claimed that hostility lay not far below the surface. More evident was Mary's extreme anxiety about her mother, who was struggling with illness and fighting to retain control of Scotland during 1559 and the first half of 1560. The nobility in Scotland had been growing restless under the regent for some time. Although Marie had included in her government the small number of Scottish nobles who were Protestant, they did not trust her and banded together as the 'Lords of the Congregation of Christ' in December 1557. By May 1559 they had become more assertive in their demands for religious change, probably

inspired by the return from exile of the pugnacious preacher John Knox. At the same time, they prepared for militant action in the hope of receiving aid from the new Protestant regime in England. During the summer the forces of the 'Congregation' went on the offensive, and Marie de Guise had to ask for military aid from France. In August and September 1559 about eighteen hundred soldiers arrived from France to suppress the Protestant revolt, but the Scottish lords continued their resistance. On 21 October they occupied Edinburgh and deposed Marie, who again appealed to France for help. In response to these pleas, her brothers arranged for French reinforcements to be sent to Scotland under the command of another member of their clan, their younger brother René, Marquis of Elbeuf, but his expedition had to be postponed because of bad weather. In the meantime, the regent's military position improved, and in December she was able to re-enter Edinburgh. The reprieve, however, was short-lived, as Elizabeth I stepped in on behalf of the rebels.

Fearful that the presence of a sizeable French army in Scotland and the defeat of the Scottish Protestants might be part of a wider scheme to put Mary Queen of Scots on the throne of England, Elizabeth I had as early as August 1559 provided the Scottish lords with £3,000. When she learnt of Elbeuf's rescue mission, she stepped up her aid and ordered Admiral Winter to the Firth of Forth with instructions to blockade the port of Leith and prevent the embarkation of French troops.

ELIZABETH   REGINA

Elizabeth and Mary: the Early Years

Portrait of Queen Elizabeth I, c.1560 by an unknown artist. When this portrait was painted, Elizabeth was fearful that Mary intended to claim her throne.
(National Portrait Gallery, London)

Portrait of Sir Nicholas Throckmorton, c.1562 by an unknown artist. While ambassador to France, Sir Nicholas Throckmorton saw Mary on several occasions and reported back to England on her appearance, health and ambitions. Following Elizabeth's instructions, he tried unsuccessfully to persuade Mary to ratify the Treaty of Edinburgh, which denied her the right to bear the arms of England.
(National Portrait Gallery, London)

Although the French reinforcements never arrived, as they were dispersed by violent storms in January 1560, Elizabeth decided, albeit reluctantly, to give military aid to the Scottish rebels. On 22 February she signed the Treaty of Berwick, committing herself to send troops over the border, and in March an army under Lord Grey besieged Leith, where it met dogged resistance from the French garrison there.

In her military intervention, Elizabeth had only limited objectives: the removal of French troops from Scotland and the security of the Protestant lords. Her principal secretary, William Cecil, however, had a more ambitious agenda: he wanted the deposition of Mary. In her place he preferred to see a Protestant union of England and Scotland under Elizabeth, but was prepared to settle for the Scottish crown to be transferred to Mary's heir, the Duke of Châtelherault, or to her illegitimate half-brother, Lord James Stewart, who had led the rebels from the start. Elizabeth, however, would not contemplate such a radical solution, and the Scottish Protestants also drew back from Mary's deposition. They had no wish for union with England, and also could not agree on a successor.

The Guises proved helpless once the English had invaded. Not only did bad weather foil their attempts to send troops to Scotland, but political events in France were also turning against them. Their power was being undermined by Catherine de' Medici and the princes of the blood, while in early March a Protestant plot was uncovered, which had been designed to oust the duke and cardinal from power and bring about a palace revolution. Guise ambitions in Scotland, therefore, ceased to be a high priority, and no further troops were sent to relieve the garrison at Leith.

Mary watched these events unfold with increasing despair, offering her mother hope and promising help that was out of her control to provide. By April 1560 it all seemed too much for her. According to Throckmorton, 'the French Queen made very great lamentations, and wept bitterly and as it is reported said that her uncles had undone her and caused her to lose her realm'.[21] Worse was to come. Marie de Guise fell seriously ill at the beginning of June, and on 11 June 1560 she died. Knowing that it would grieve her terribly, her uncles kept the news from Mary for ten days after they first heard it. When informed, she was inconsolable; according to the Venetian ambassador, she 'passed from one agony to another'.[22]

Soon after her mother's death, Mary had to accept defeat in Scotland. Behind her back, the Guises agreed to the Treaty of Edinburgh, which was signed by French, Scottish and English commissioners on 6 July 1560. By its terms the Guises not only accepted the evacuation of French troops from Scotland, but also recognized the title of Elizabeth to the English throne by agreeing that Mary would no longer use the arms of England. Henceforth Scotland was to be ruled by a council consisting of seven or eight members selected by Mary, and five or six by parliament. Although nominally the Queen of Scotland, Mary took no part in the negotiations, nor did she agree to the terms of the treaty – she had been completely bypassed and consequently considered the treaty illegal.

Now, for the first time, Mary took an independent line in policy. She and her husband would not ratify the Treaty of Edinburgh. Furthermore, she continued to use the arms of England, despite its prohibition in the treaty. When Throckmorton arrived at Orléans to be with the royal court in November 1560, he found that the king bore her arms quartered with his own 'openly upon every gate [of this town], and here at the court gate very notoriously'.[23] Later on, Mary was to say that she merely followed the will of her husband, but it is questionable whether the immature François had a will of his own in political life.

While hunting near Orléans in mid-November 1560, François caught a chill. His health had never been good, and he was frequently afflicted with respiratory and ear infections. But on this occasion he had an ear infection that was sufficiently grave for the doctors to fear he would not survive. The infection soon spread to the brain, where it formed an abscess. Mary and Catherine stayed by his bedside, watching and nursing the sick king as he lay in agony. On 5 December, shortly before his seventeenth birthday, François died. Mary immediately left the royal apartments and went into mourning. Following traditional

rituals, she withdrew into a darkened chamber for forty days. For the first fifteen of them she allowed no man into the room, except those of highest standing – the new king, his brothers and her closest relatives. On the last day of the mourning period, she attended a solemn requiem for her late husband at the Greyfriars' church in Orléans. Her demeanour at this time attracted positive comment. Even Throckmorton declared that she showed herself to be 'of great wisdom for her years, modesty, and also of great judgement in the wise handling herself and her matters'.[24]

Immediately after her husband's death, Mary lost her status as Queen of France, and consideration was given to her future. On 6 December she had to hand over her crown jewels to Catherine, who organized an inventory of them. On 20 December the jointure stipulated in her marriage contract was confirmed, and it was agreed that she would receive the sizeable annual income of 60,000 livres tournois from estates in France. Even before her husband's burial, talk began of her remarriage, and the names of many candidates were mentioned. Mary, however, seems to have put aside all thoughts of marriage at this date. She may have initially toyed with the idea of a marriage to the new French king, Charles IX, or to Philip II's son, Don Carlos, but it is more likely that the Guises were the ones keen on her embarking on a prestigious and influential foreign match. Mary's preference was to return to Scotland before deciding on a new husband. In January 1561 she sent envoys to Scotland to inform the

lords there of her wish for a continuation of the old alliance with France, and to arrange for money to be sent to pay for her journey home. Mary's decision has often been considered rather strange, as she was so French in her manners and outlook and had no friends in Scotland. But Mary may well have craved full independence and power after years under the close supervision and control of the Guise family.

Now that François II was dead, Elizabeth I hoped that Mary could be persuaded to sign the Treaty of Edinburgh. Consequently, she quickly dispatched the Earl of Bedford to France to offer her condolences, and to insist on the treaty's ratification. Bedford and the resident English ambassador were granted access to Mary on 16 February 1561, but her response disappointed them. Although she professed her desire for friendship with the English queen, she prevaricated about the treaty, claiming she could not sign it without first taking counsel from her subjects.

On several more occasions, Throckmorton pressed her to approve the treaty, but Mary remained resolutely evasive. As a result, Elizabeth became aggrieved and very suspicious of her cousin, fearing that she had designs on the English throne.

In March 1561 Mary left the court to visit and say goodbye to her Guise relations and personal friends before embarking for Scotland. She had planned to attend Charles IX's coronation on Ascension Day (15 May), but a bout of tertian ague (a form of malaria) laid her low and put paid to that plan. While on her travels, she was visited by rival Scottish envoys, who were each keen to offer her advice and win her over to their side. Her half-brother Lord James Stewart spoke for the Lords of the Congregation, then in power, and urged Mary to accept the new Protestant settlement that had been introduced in Scotland in August 1560; in return, he promised that she could have the Mass celebrated within her household. The Catholic faction was represented by John Leslie, the future Bishop of Ross, who recommended that the queen should join forces with the leading Catholic nobleman George Gordon, 4th Earl of Huntly, to dismantle the Reformed Church and subjugate the Protestants.

It did not take Mary long to decide to align herself with the Protestant lords rather than risk a confrontation that could lead only to a civil war that she might well lose. She was prepared to forgive the lords for their rebellion against her mother and to give them

OPPOSITE

*Portrait of Lord James Stewart, c.*1565 by an unknown artist. In 1559 Mary's illegitimate half-brother James led the Protestant Lords of the Congregation against the government of Marie de Guise. After acting for several years as Mary's adviser, he became a fierce opponent of her and Darnley. He took up the position of regent on her abdication.
(Lennoxlove House Ltd)

assurances that she would not mount a counter-reformation. At the same time she clearly found the new ecclesiastical order in Scotland distasteful. As far as she was concerned, the lords and parliament had had no legal authority to break with Rome, abolish the Mass and reorganize the Church. Furthermore, she had no intention of converting to Protestantism. As she announced to Throckmorton: 'The religion that I profess I take to be most acceptable to God and, indeed, neither do I know, nor desire to know, any other'.[25] The informal agreement reached with Lord James was that she would recognize the Reformed Church, but hear the Mass in her chapel.

Mary returned to Paris on 10 June 1561, and on 20 July a farewell feast, lasting four days, was held at Saint-Germain in her honour. She intended to journey to Scotland by sea, but requested a safe conduct from Elizabeth in case she was forced by bad weather or illness to land in England. To her surprise, Elizabeth refused the passport unless Mary first ratified the Treaty of Edinburgh. Although clearly angry at this discourtesy, Mary kept control of her temper and retained her dignity in her last few interviews with Throckmorton. Taking the moral high ground, she accused Elizabeth of preferring to offer friendship to rebels than to their sovereign queen. She also denied that she intended any harm to Elizabeth by waiting to receive counsel from Scotland before signing the treaty. Her goodwill, she declared, had already been demonstrated in that she had ceased to bear the arms of England as soon as

her husband had died. In this early duel between the two queens, Mary's behaviour could hardly be faulted, whereas that of Elizabeth could be (and was) criticized as small-minded and unfriendly. Implicitly acknowledging this, the English queen backed down and wrote her cousin a friendly letter denying that she had any intention of 'impeaching' her crossing. But this safe conduct arrived too late for Mary's use.

Mary left Calais on 14 August 1561 with three ships and a few dozen companions and servants. Amongst those on board her own ship were the four Maries and three of her Guise uncles, who were to act as escorts on the journey. The other ships were laden with Mary's possessions: her wardrobe, furniture, tapestries, Turkish carpets, gold and silver plate and a horse-drawn litter. On this voyage Mary showed little of the excitement she had displayed on her passage to France thirteen years previously. Instead she wept while looking backwards to France, repeating mournfully, 'Adieu France, adieu France, adieu donc ma chère France,' adding at least once, 'It's all over now. Adieu France. I think I'll never see your shores again.'[26] She was right.

Copied by W. Penny from an Engraving in the possession.
of the Society of Antiquaries, of Scotland.

CHAPTER THREE
Widowed Queen of Scotland
1561–1564

MARY LANDED AT Leith in Scotland on Tuesday 19 August 1561, after only five days at sea. She arrived on a dank, foggy morning, a week earlier than expected. No one was waiting for her; no horses stood by to convey her to Edinburgh; and Holyrood Palace was not quite ready. But soon after this inauspicious start to her homecoming, she was welcomed properly: the nobility came out to greet her and bonfires were lit in Edinburgh. That evening she settled into the royal apartments in the north-west tower of Holyrood, where she was kept awake by a group of her enthusiastic subjects who boisterously sang and played the fiddle and rebec beneath her window throughout the night. Perhaps thankful for signs of celebration, Mary told them charmingly the next morning that she willed 'the same to be continued some nights after'.[27]

No sooner had Mary arrived than her religion became a matter of contention. On the first Sunday she spent at Holyrood, a mob of Calvinist zealots noisily protested when she and her household prepared to attend Mass. Only the presence of Lord James Stewart and two more of her Protestant half-brothers kept them from bursting into the private chapel and manhandling the priest.

OPPOSITE
Portrait of Mary Queen of Scots, c.1560–5 by an unknown artist.
(National Portrait Gallery, London)

The next day, 25 August, Mary tried to reassure her Protestant subjects by issuing a proclamation that endorsed the religious situation then in place. At the same time, she commanded that no one should molest her domestic servants or company from France in the practice of their religion. The following Sunday John Knox, the fiery Scottish Calvinist preacher at St Giles, denounced the Mass from the pulpit, and just over a week later, on Tuesday 2 September, the Protestant leaders of the city used the occasion of Mary's royal entry into Edinburgh to signal their dislike of her religion.

The first part of Mary's entry – her procession into Edinburgh and the banquet in the castle for the civic leaders of the town – passed without controversy and was well attended by Protestants and Catholics alike. But as the procession made its return towards Holyrood, a number of contentious pageants were staged before the queen. In one of them a small boy descended from a mechanical globe, as if an angel from heaven, and presented Mary with two gifts – a Bible covered with purple velvet, and a psalter – which he explained were most worthy for a godly prince or, in other words, for a Protestant ruler who would advance the Gospel. With a frown Mary handed them to her Catholic captain of the guard and moved on quickly. Another tableau depicted a Catholic priest burnt at the altar while elevating the Host, but it was stopped by the Catholic Earl of Huntly walking at the front of the procession before Mary could see it. Hastily, another scene was enacted in which effigies of three

Israelites were burnt for defying Moses. As this could be taken as an allegory against idolatry or blasphemy, it offended neither the Protestants nor Catholics. The final pageant, showing a papier mâché dragon set on fire while a psalm was sung, was probably intended as an allusion to the downfall of popery; and in the closing moments of the procession Mary was forced to hear another child singing a psalm and reciting verses that attacked the Mass.

On the morning of 4 September 1561 Mary held the first of four personal interviews with John Knox, where, predictably, there was no meeting of minds. Mary had no wish to debate theology with Knox because, as she admitted, she did not have the knowledge to answer his points. Knox, however, subjected his queen to a lengthy and vehement diatribe on the nature of true religion. When Mary criticized him for his condemnation of women rulers in the 1558 book *The First Blast of the Trumpet against the Monstrous Regiment of Women*, and for inciting her subjects against Marie de Guise, Knox declared his readiness to obey Mary as St Paul had obeyed Nero. Given that Nero had been a notorious tyrant and persecutor of Christians, this comment was a deliberate provocation. Not stopping there, Knox went on to defend his radical view that subjects had the right to resist rulers who disobeyed the word of God. Mary was apparently flabbergasted, both at Knox's bluntness and his challenge to monarchical authority. According to Knox, she remained silent for 'more than the quarter of an hour' before replying: 'Well, then, I perceive

that my subjects shall obey you, and not me; and shall do what they list, and not what I command: so must I be subject to them, and not they to me.'[28] After telling Mary that she was ignorant of the Scriptures, the preacher departed and the queen burst into tears. The interview was partially overheard by Lord James Stewart, who, like most of Mary's other Protestant councillors, disapproved of this harangue and high-handed treatment of the queen.

Despite the hostility of Knox and a few other Protestant die-hards, Mary kept to her agreement with Lord James Stewart, and did nothing to weaken the Protestants in power, and very little to endanger the Reformed Church. She retained the Protestant government ministers she had inherited, and appointed all the leading Protestant Lords of

ABOVE
Illustration of John Knox, from *An oration against the unlawfull protestantes insurrections of our time under pretence to reforme religion*, a book produced in Antwerp in 1566. In 1558 the Protestant preacher and Mary's opponent wrote *The First Blast of the Trumpet against the Monstrous Regiment of Women*, and is here shown blowing it against her. The Protestant Christopher Goodman is blowing a similar trumpet against Mary I of England. (British Library, C.37.d.47)

OVERLEAF
Commission from Mary to William Maitland of Lethington to treat with the English government, 24 May 1562. This was to be Maitland's second embassy to England, and its main purpose was to arrange an interview between the two queens. In 1563 he returned to England to raise the question of the succession. (British Library, Egerton 1818, Latin copy, f. 20)

Maria dei gra Regina Scotorum Gallie Dotaria Universis a-
quos presentes lre pervenerint Notum facimus q[uo]d cu[m] post nrm in
Scotiam reditum omni studio semp[er] id contenderimus ut cu[m] charissim[a]
sorore nra et consanguinea Anglie regina benevolentia [illegible]
certiore et charitate qua et utriusque regni utilitas et [illegible]
tranquillitas et omnis in quo posita semper loci nos populabat [illegible]
in eam amor neque tanta animi constantia neque illius de nob[is]
mutuis mutuisque literarum testimoniis contentus esse poterat nisi
ultro etiam satisfaceret nobis cupiebamus cum et etiam [illegible]
coram illi declarare quanto tranquillitati publice quanto il-
liusque tranquillitati semper faverimus hinc nos studio tanto
etiamque nulla de nos congressu fieri posse videretur aspectu
publico tu interesse putabamus ut de amore nostro constantia
et animis et dum sibi colloquio fieret illustrior ut
alteri nobiscum in publica commoda faverent et in futurum
confirmarentur Alteri si qua turbande nre concordie ser-
vanda cogitassent eam prorsus abiicerent. Simul illud co-
gitabamus multa per colloquium facilius transigi posse quam per
literas ut non modo presentia si qua sunt mala sanarentur
sed etiam inventa salubri consilio precavendo avertentur. Ea[m]
de causam cum charissima quoque soror nra in eandem sententiam
venerit animadvertimus dilectum et fidelem consiliarium nrm
Gulielmum Matlande de Lethington secretarium nrm primarium
ad eam mittendum designavimus de tempore et loco totaque co-
lloquii congressus [illegible] ratione id illa agerent de cuius quidem
industria integritate et erga nos fide plurimum confidentes
eum in hoc negotio tenore presentium nrm facimus constituimus
et creamus commissarium legatum et oratorem dantes et conce-
dentes eidem nro commissario et oratori nram plenam et liberam
potestatem pro nobis et noie nro omnia et singula tractandi
concludendi promittendi et concludendi que ad tempus et locum oppor-
tunitates vel alias ad dictum nrm colloquium spectare que-
modo poterunt vel illi et necessaria videbuntur et oportuna
etiam si talia sint que mandatum exigant magis speciale
Promittentes bona fide et verbo regio ratum et gratum
habere et habituram totum id quod dictus nr commissarius et
orator in premissis duxerit faciendum In cuius rei testi-
monium presentibus manu nra subscriptis sigillum nrm magnum
apponi fecimus Apud Edinburgh vicesimo quarto mensis
maii Ao 1562. et regni nri vicesimo.

the Congregation to her council, including Lord James, who in early 1562 was made Earl of Moray, a title traditionally held by members of the royal family. It is true that she protected Catholics within Edinburgh from persecution, and also deferred ratification of the parliamentary statute of August 1560 that had abolished the Mass; but she did nothing to stop the arrest of priests who celebrated Mass outside her own chapel at Holyrood, sent no Scottish deputation to attend the last session of the papal Council of Trent, and dismissed as 'impracticable' the pope's suggestion that a Catholic seminary be established in Scotland. In 1562, moreover, she approved arrangements that put the new Reformed Kirk on a more secure financial basis.

PREVIOUS PAGE
Portrait of William Maitland of Lethington, c.1560(?). He was appointed Mary's secretary of state in 1561 and used by her in negotiations with Elizabeth. His second wife was Mary Fleming, one of the 'four Maries' (see page 26). (Lennoxlove House Ltd)

Mary's religious policy contrasts strongly with that of both Mary I and Elizabeth I, who sought to impose their personal religion on England. It is possible that a policy of moderation suited Mary's temperament. As she had explained to Throckmorton, 'I mean to constrain none of my subjects, but would wish they were all as I am.'[29] But political considerations may also have influenced her behaviour. She evidently thought that an acceptance of the Protestant status quo was the best way to avoid political instability, even civil war. In this respect her approach was similar to that of her mother and Catherine de' Medici. Additionally, Mary had yet another motive for working co-operatively with the Protestant regime in Scotland. As will soon be shown, her long-term ambitions were focused on England, and her heart was set on winning the succession to the throne of Elizabeth. By choosing Protestant councillors, she could reassure English politicians that her succession after Elizabeth need not involve a political revolution. Refusing to promote Catholicism in Scotland was, likewise, a calculated move to show the wider group of English Protestants that they had no need to fear for the future of their Church on her future accession.

But first Mary had to negotiate with Elizabeth. At this point Mary was prepared to hold back from challenging Elizabeth's title to the English throne if, in return, the childless Elizabeth would acknowledge her right to the succession and name her as heir presumptive. Although next in line by blood to the English throne, Mary feared that without this formal recognition, English Protestants might seek to prevent her future accession by exploiting two legalistic impediments to her legitimate claim. The first impediment was Henry VIII's will in which he had left the throne to the descendants of his younger sister, if his direct line died out, and not to those of his elder sister (Mary's grandmother). The second was a ruling in English common law that aliens could not inherit property in England. Neither of these bars was undisputed, but they could certainly be used against Mary's future title. Mary was also concerned that the 1560 Treaty of Edinburgh further weakened her claim to the succession, since one of its terms demanded that she should cease styling herself Queen of England. This article, Mary argued, might be interpreted as a renunciation of her rights to the English throne even after Elizabeth's death. Consequently, Mary wanted the treaty renegotiated to exclude that possibility. Following the advice of Lord James Stewart and William Maitland of Lethington, her policy was to persuade Elizabeth to recognize her as heir and in return she would renounce her claim to the English throne during Elizabeth's lifetime.

In September 1561, barely two weeks after her arrival in Scotland, Maitland of Lethington was dispatched to London to negotiate the succession issue. He offered a deal in which Mary would sign a revised treaty in return for Elizabeth's recognition of her as legal heir. Maitland's mission, however, proved unsuccessful. Although Elizabeth indicated

that she favoured Mary's claim to the succession, she refused point blank to name an heir on several different grounds. First, designating her heir would be politically dangerous since conspiracies were likely to surround her or him. Second, as she explained frankly to Maitland, her relations with Mary would deteriorate rather than improve were the Scottish queen to be named her successor. 'Princes cannot like their own children,' she said. 'How then shall I, think you, like my cousin, being declared my heir apparent?'[30] Third, the issue of the succession was divisive and Elizabeth did not want it to become a subject of public debate. As she well knew, Mary was an unpopular candidate because of her religion, nationality and links with the Guises. Many at Elizabeth's court, including William Cecil, far preferred the claim of Katherine Grey, the Protestant granddaughter of Henry VIII's younger sister, or even the Earl of Huntingdon, whose descent went back to Edward III. But although Elizabeth would not settle the succession, she did consider reviewing the terms of the Treaty of Edinburgh so that Mary would not have to sign away any future claim to the throne, and Maitland returned home satisfied at least on that point. Towards the end of November, however, Elizabeth changed her mind and called on Mary to ratify the original treaty.

Disappointed at this outcome, Mary pinned her hopes on arranging a face-to-face meeting with her cousin where good will could be built up. At a personal interview, Mary told Elizabeth, 'we trust you shall more clearly

will in hir mariage have regard to these thyngs, and content
and this owr nation in hir mariage, uppon assured knoliege
to procede to y nomynacion of hir right or title to be owr next cozyn
heyre, and to furder that which shall appeare avantageous for
and to hynder and impeache that which shall seme to
contrary, using also therin such meanes as may be ____ to the ___
tion of owr realme, both owr nobilitie and Comons.

And if she shall press uppon yow what kynd of mariage yow thynk might
best content us and owr realme, ye may well, it seme y ___ ___
such as may not be ____ to us or owr people, that it is ___
sought, to procure trooble to this realme, as ther ___ was doone in
tyme of hir mariage to y french kyng. And therfor ye maye saye
cam but wish that ther might be found some noble person of gre
byrth within this owr realme, that might be agreable to hir, or if th
shall not be, yet of some other contrye, being one who nether we nor owr ___
shuld have manifest cause to indg to be sought for y trooble of this re
and than might we more redyly and easely, shew and extend the
will that we have to y furderace of owr Sister, and otherwise ye ___
playnely saye, we can promiss nothyng agreable to y fervet desyre that ___
bewr to doo hir good, which is of owr owne natwrall disposition, to ha
hir to enioye before any creatwr any thyng that we have, next to ___
self, or if god shall so order us to have any: and this yow may ___
we asswre hir at this tyme is owr desyre unfaynedly.

Mary and Marriage

Letter from Elizabeth I to Thomas Randolph, dated 20 August 1563, in which she makes recommendations about whom Mary should marry. Elizabeth has heard rumours that Mary is thinking of marrying a member of the powerful Habsburg family, and here she instructs Randolph, her ambassador in Scotland, about what to tell Mary. He is to explain to her that such a marriage would be interpreted as a hostile act (see paragraph two):

'And if she shall press upon you what kind of marriage you think might best content us and our realm, ye may well say that it must be such, as may not be apparent to us or our people, that it is only sought to procure trouble to this realm as she saw was done in the time of her marriage to the French king. And therefore ye may say ye can but wish that there might be found some noble person of great birth within this our realm, that might be agreeable to her.'

She goes on to say that if Mary still decides to choose a foreigner as her husband, he must be someone 'who neither we nor our realm should have manifest cause to judge to be sought for the trouble of this realm'. In her final sentence Elizabeth leaves open the possibility that she might herself marry and 'if God shall so order' have children. The letter, although signed by Elizabeth, is in the handwriting of her minister Sir William Cecil. (British Library, Cotton Caligula B X, f. 219v)

LEFT

Portrait of Lord Henry Darnley, c.1565 by an unknown artist. Mary's cousin and second husband looks somewhat effeminate in this portrait, painted when he was about twenty years old, but his elegance and beauty are unmistakable. (Scottish National Portrait Gallery)

ABOVE

Darnley's love poem to Mary, 'My hope is yow for to obtaine', 1565(?). (British Library, Additional MS 17492, f. 57) perceive the sincerity of our good meaning than we can express by writing'.[31] In fact, in the summer of 1561 Elizabeth had already offered to meet Mary in return for the ratification of the Treaty of Edinburgh. Now, in 1562, Mary was to run with the idea in order to effect its renegotiation.

During the spring and early summer of 1562, Mary's relationship with Elizabeth improved greatly. Elizabeth responded positively to the idea of a personal interview, and plans were soon laid for a meeting in York or Nottingham, either in August or September. Elizabeth also began to write regularly to her cousin, her correspondence emphasizing their family relationship. Delighted at the prospect of reconciliation, Mary had specially made for Elizabeth a miniature portrait set in a ring behind a large diamond framed like a heart as a token of love and friendship. Elizabeth reciprocated with a portrait sent in June 1562 and a ring the following year. Meanwhile, the two queens exchanged verses they had written, though because of her difficulties with Latin Mary received help with two of hers from the humanist scholar George Buchanan, who was then employed as an informal tutor in Latin.

By the end of June 1562, however, Elizabeth's advisers were having second thoughts about the meeting. Cecil had probably always objected to it, but events abroad now convinced him and the entire English Privy Council that it should be postponed. The previous March, Mary's uncle the Duke of Guise and his retinue had massacred a congregation of Protestants at prayer in the village of Vassy, and civil war had erupted in France the following month. As the French Protestants were seeking help from England against the Catholics led by the Guises, it was an inopportune time for the two queens to meet. An interview, argued Cecil, would in these circumstances boost the Guises' 'credit in France', while Mary would exploit her journey into England to 'insinuate herself to some sorts of people of this realm to further her claim' to the throne.[32] Despite this advice, Elizabeth initially decided to go ahead with the meeting. Taking advantage of a ceasefire in France, she confirmed on 6 July 1562 that York, midway between Edinburgh and London, would be the venue. Generously, Mary and her retinue were to be allowed 'to use the rites and ceremonies of their religion as at this day they use in Scotland';[33] less generously, she was expected to pay her own expenses. Six days later, however, the French returned to war, and Elizabeth consequently postponed the interview until the following year. On hearing the news, Mary was not simply disappointed, but distraught. According to the English envoy, she fell 'into such a passion as she did keep her bed all that day', refusing to move or speak to anyone.[34]

With the interview postponed, Mary decided to go on progress to the Highlands. Earlier in the year she had planned to visit the north-eastern part of her realm to display herself to her subjects, but the project had been shelved in favour of the meeting with Elizabeth. Mary was now free to travel, and by August 1562 another motive had emerged for a journey to the north. Mary wanted to confront the Catholic Earl of Huntly, who held extensive lands and powerful interests in the region. Although she had confirmed him as chancellor on her arrival in Scotland, the earl soon quarrelled with Lord James Stewart and made known his disapproval of Mary's policies; in the spring of 1562 he even stopped attending council meetings. Huntly firmly opposed the meeting with Elizabeth, consistently displayed pro-French sympathies and expressed deep disappointment with Mary's religious policy. Mary intended to bring the earl into line during her progress, and by this means hoped both to silence an outspoken critic and demonstrate to Elizabeth her sincerity in professing friendship towards England. So that this message would reach the English queen, Thomas Randolph, her ambassador, was asked to join Mary on the progress.

From the start of her journey, Mary showed her displeasure with Huntly. At Aberdeen she listened coolly to Lady Elizabeth Huntly's plea that she pardon their son, Sir John Gordon, who had recently assaulted one of her lords and dispossessed another of his inheritance. Mary then rejected the invitation to stay at Huntly's splendid seat at Strathbogie on her way to Inverness, and a little later at Darnaway Castle she bestowed on Lord James Stewart the earldom of Moray, which Huntly had administered for the Crown over several years. In the face of this evident hostility from the queen, Huntly showed defiance, not submission. When welcoming Mary at

Aberdeen, he had turned up with fifteen hundred retainers, although ordered to bring no more than a hundred. Far worse, when Mary arrived at Inverness on 11 September, one of his captains refused her entry into the castle, forcing her to lodge in the town. The queen, however, quickly rallied troops amongst the Highlanders and took the castle the next day. There she ordered the captain to be hanged from the battlements. Huntly, however, still roamed free, while Sir John Gordon laid plans to abduct Mary on her way back to Aberdeen. Far from being scared by this adventure, Mary was resilient, even elated: 'In all these garboils,' wrote Randolph, 'I never saw her merrier, never dismayed, nor never thought that stomach to be in her that I find!'[35]

Although Huntly protested his loyalty to the queen, he refused to hand over his son or submit to her will. Consequently, in October 1562, Mary had little choice but to declare him an outlaw, and on 28 October a royal army led by Moray encircled Huntly's force near Aberdeen. In the ensuing battle of Corrichie, the rebels were decisively beaten. The earl was captured, but suffered a stroke and died before being led off the battlefield. Sir John and other rebels were beheaded in the presence of Mary, who, according to some later accounts, broke down and wept when the executioner bungled the job. John's elder brother, George, who had not been present at the battle, was spared, but he was kept in custody and all his father's lands and titles were confiscated by the Crown. Some of the earl's local offices were then given to Lord James, the Earl of Moray.

Historians are divided over whether or not Mary's policy towards Huntly was fair and wise. While a few, including Maurice Lee, see her action as the successful and legitimate assertion of royal authority, others, notably Jenny Wormald, argue more convincingly that her treatment of the Gordon family was exceptionally harsh by Scottish standards and threw the region into confusion. In the long term, the wholesale forfeiture of Gordon lands disrupted the long-accepted relationship between Crown and nobility, and encouraged their disobedience against her later in the reign. Additionally, by giving Moray a power base in the north, Mary created a factional rivalry between the Gordon and Stewart families that would cause problems during the reign of her son. In the short term, moreover, Mary failed to take advantage of Huntly's demise to bring the north-east under royal control, and made no consistent attempt to dismantle the infrastructure of Gordon power. Naturally, she also made no attempt to impose Protestantism on the region.

In an embassy to England, Maitland presented Mary's policy towards Huntly as evidence that English Protestants need have no fears that Mary would favour Catholics were she to be accepted as Elizabeth's successor. Cecil, however, remained suspicious and hostile. When Elizabeth was struck down with smallpox in October 1562, he and some other members of the Privy Council refused to consider Mary as heir. Furthermore, in the parliament of January 1563, he worked with friends to present a petition to the queen,

which was designed to exclude Mary from the succession. When Mary learnt of these attempts to deprive her of her rights, she was so distressed that she apparently fell ill for six days. At that time she could not know that Elizabeth would reject the parliamentary petition and prevent her exclusion from the succession. All Mary could see was that her plans for a personal meeting with Elizabeth had slipped off the political agenda (ostensibly because of England's military involvement in the civil war in France) and that opposition to her succession was growing in England. In these circumstances, Mary had little incentive to continue her policy of appeasement towards Elizabeth. For that reason she turned her thoughts towards a second marriage and began her search for a husband who would uphold her right to the English succession, even though he might not be to Elizabeth's liking.

I wrote so lately vnto yo[ur] L[ordship] that there reste[th] none nothynge to be reported of. The lre [letter] that I heretofore desired sholde come vnto yo[ur] handes I sent vnto mr Killigrewe. yt beare the date the laste of ffebruarie. That I wrote by it come is but to smale effecte, rather to haue byen occasion to see yo[ur] L[ordship] then that I had anye matter to wryte of. This bearers diligence hathe byen so greate in searchynge forthe the state of thynge here that his reporte therof is no lesse assured then anye thynge that I cann wryte. his good wyll vnto yo[ur] L[ordship] suche that I am righte certayne that he wyll as largelye and openlye deale with yo[ur] L[ordship] in reportynge the veritie of all thynge as to anye frende he hathe. I wyll not therfore trouble yo[ur] L[ordship] with anye thynge that I thinke that he cann speake of, but rather searche some other matter of whic[h] perhapps so meane yt be, to acquaynt thys lytle wyne that I haue gotten more then thys daye I looked for, by reason that so morerowe I thought to haue followed the q[ue]ne to ... did wonb, and nome obys the comynge of some one or other whome latlye I harde of that sholde brynge vnto thys Quene my mistres picture whom I receyue to receaue and to ...

I looke also at that tyme to here of the lyklyhood of the interviewe of the two Quenes then yet I do. whear vpon we are here all readye so farre aseled, that vpon the reporte answer that comith from thence, the L[ordship] of huntyngton is lyke to take his journeye to the Quenes ma[ies]tie to declare vnto Quene his mistres good wyll and to desyre that yt maye be founde good that they maye mete, with other mistr famous with yo[ur] L[ordship] cann as well geshen or comiertence as we. I am wryte of thys matters yt is necessarie that yo[ur] L[ordship] sholde be made previe. I wryte yt notwythstandynge vnto yo[ur] L[ordship] as a Conseller fitter to be knowne to yo[ur] selfe then anye many els, but at yo[ur] disore. There is prepared here to be sent vnto my mistres by him that brynge the here picture a ringe with a diemonde framed by...

Mary had much to offer as the bride of a foreign prince: her charm and beauty were renowned, while her wealth and domains could be considered added attractions. But she had a rival in Elizabeth, who was still unmarried, and many potential foreign suitors for Mary were already seeking the hand of the English queen, or had no wish to offend her by marrying a pretender to the English throne. Mary's first choice of bridegroom was Don Carlos, the seventeen-year-old heir of Philip II. Marriage to him would not only place Mary once again on the international stage and add to her reputation, wealth and prestige, but, more importantly, an alliance with Spain would provide the necessary political and military muscle to pursue her claim to the English throne. In February 1563 Maitland of Lethington discussed the match with the Spanish ambassador at Elizabeth's court, but Philip II was not enthusiastic. Philip did, however, allow the matrimonial discussions to proceed secretly as he feared Mary might make overtures of marriage to the young French king, Charles IX, instead.

News of the Spanish negotiations soon leaked out and naturally caused consternation in Scotland, France and England. In Scotland Knox vigorously condemned the very notion of a Catholic marriage, first from the pulpit and then to Mary's face, causing the queen to howl and weep 'in a vehement fume' while in his presence.[36] In France Catherine de' Medici and the Cardinal of Lorraine tried to deflect Mary's plans. Catherine refused to countenance her own son as an alternative bridegroom, but

encouraged the cardinal to open up a parallel set of negotiations for a match with the Habsburg Emperor Ferdinand's son, Archduke Charles of Austria. Mary, however, dismissed this suggestion because the archduke had neither the wealth nor status to suit her interests. As far as Elizabeth and Cecil were concerned, both the Spanish and Austrian candidates were equally unacceptable. The Habsburgs, they feared, would put their weight behind a papal excommunication of Elizabeth, encourage a Catholic rebellion in the realm, and quite possibly launch an invasion to put Mary on the English throne.

In June 1563 the English queen notified Maitland that she would be forced to regard Mary as an enemy if either a Spanish or imperial match were agreed. In August Randolph was instructed to inform Mary that any such marriage would be viewed as an unfriendly act and jeopardize her chances of being recognized as heir presumptive. As an alternative, Elizabeth recommended that Mary marry 'some noble person of great birth within our realm' or possibly a foreigner who would pose no 'trouble to our realm' and threat to their 'amity' (see page 68). Mary listened coolly to these warnings and suggestions, and then politely asked Elizabeth to identify a person who might be considered a suitable husband. In response, Elizabeth did not provide a name but simply repeated her criteria: ideally, Mary should marry an English Protestant nobleman, and, if she did so, her right to the English succession would be investigated. But if Mary chose instead to make a foreign match, it was not to be with one of 'the children of France, Spain or Austria'. In this communication Mary could scarcely have failed to notice that Elizabeth was not promising to acknowledge her right to the succession, but only offering to open up an enquiry into her claim, which was hardly a satisfactory concession. Mary may also have been aware that the English Protestant nobleman preferred by Elizabeth was Lord Robert Dudley, for his name had already been mentioned to Maitland the previous spring. If so, Mary probably dismissed the thought, for the offer of Dudley was little more than insulting. As yet he had no noble title, and, besides, he had been romantically linked with Elizabeth since 1559. Indeed, the scandal of their relationship had first amused the French court and then shocked it when rumours circulated after September 1560 that he had murdered his wife in order to clear the way for a marriage to Elizabeth.

For some months Mary was left to guess at Elizabeth's meaning. She tried to tease a name out of Randolph, but with no success, although he did drop some broad hints. At last, on 5 March 1564, Mary asked outright who it was that Elizabeth wanted her to marry. When she was told officially that it was Dudley, she heard Randolph out 'with patience' and tried to contain her affront at Elizabeth's proposal that she marry her cast-off lover, who was quite possibly a murderer. Mary's dislike of the match was evident when she questioned whether marrying one of her cousin's subjects would 'stand with my honour', and suggested

that her friends 'would hardly agree that I should abase my state so far as that'. Yet, despite these strong objections, Mary was keen to learn 'what profit or commodity' she would gain by the marriage, and requested time to think about it.[37]

As preposterous as Elizabeth's proposal has seemed to many historians, both she and Mary evidently took it seriously. From Elizabeth's point of view, a Dudley match would have the merit of cementing Anglo-Scottish amity, while Dudley himself, she believed (perhaps naively), would work in the English interest to hold in check Mary's ambitions and keep her loyal to the English queen. From Mary's standpoint, marrying Dudley might just possibly be acceptable if she could thereby squeeze from Elizabeth and the English parliament recognition of her right to the succession. Besides, by mid-1564 there were few other candidates for her hand: Philip II had stalled the matrimonial negotiations with Don Carlos, who was soon to be withdrawn on the grounds of his mental instability; Charles IX of France was out of bounds; and Archduke Charles preferred the prospect of marriage to Elizabeth. Since her advisers, Moray and Maitland, favoured the Dudley marriage as the best way forward to preserve amity with England, Mary could count on their support in trying to advance it. In England, by contrast, neither Dudley nor Cecil liked the idea at all.

For several months Mary did nothing about the Dudley marriage proposal. During the summer she left the matter in abeyance while she went on progress to the far north of her realm. Then, in late September 1564, she sent to London a gentleman of her bedchamber, Sir James Melville, to ask Elizabeth to set up a conference where the match would be discussed and to ensure that the next English parliament, which was due to meet in October, did nothing to damage Mary's claim to the succession. During Melville's visit, Dudley was ennobled as Earl of Leicester in order to make him of suitable rank to wed a queen, but Elizabeth spoilt the effect of this move by allegedly tickling his neck in the midst of the ceremony.

The conference to discuss the Leicester match opened at Berwick on 18 November and was attended by Moray and Maitland for the Scots, and Randolph and Bedford for Elizabeth. At the meeting, the Scots made Mary's marriage to the earl conditional upon her parliamentary recognition as Elizabeth's heir. Elizabeth, however, would not meet this condition. Whether or not she was prepared to name her heir was immaterial; she knew there was very little likelihood that her parliament would authorize Mary's title. Consequently, she answered that Mary must rely solely on her goodwill for the fulfilment of the claim, since parliamentary ratification would not follow automatically. Elizabeth also promised that Mary's marriage to Leicester would ensure amity between the two rulers. Of course, these terms were utterly unacceptable to the Scots, and the negotiations reached an impasse. Over the next few months, Moray and Maitland put

pressure on Elizabeth to concede to Mary's demands, but to no avail.

Apart from the questions surrounding her marriage and relations with England, Mary showed little interest in political affairs and took no initiatives concerning the realm's religion, revenues or administration. Unusually for a Scottish monarch, she rarely attended council meetings, even though they were held in the royal Palace of Holyrood where she had her apartments. Her contacts with councillors were so spasmodic that a year after her return to Scotland a rota was drawn up of councillors who should attend on the queen 'by whose advice the causes of her Grace and realm may be ordered as shall be thought most commodious and profitable'.[38]

OPPOSITE

Portrait of George Buchanan, 1581 by Arnold von Bronckhorst. Buchanan acted as Mary's classical tutor and court poet for several years after 1561. Following the murder of her second husband, he turned against her and wrote *De Maria Scotorum* *Regina* (1571), which was translated as *Ane Detectioun of the Duings of Marie, Quene of Scottes...* (see pages 134–5). This portrait was painted while Buchanan was tutor to Mary's son, James VI. (National Gallery of Scotland)

By contrast, Mary chose to surround herself with Scottish courtiers, such as Lord George Seton and the Flemings, as well as household servants who were French. She had brought to Scotland several servants from France, including Gilbert de Beaucaire, Sieur de Peguillen, who acted as her master of the household, and Claude de Parcheminier, who acted as one of her secretaries. In addition, she retained several French members of her mother's household, including her comptroller Bartholomew de Villemore, and her master of the household, Jean de Bussot, as well as her apothecary, several *valets de chambre* and a secretary. Her confessor initially was the Frenchman René Benoist, who was a famous Catholic preacher and author.

Court life was vibrant under Mary. To the disgust of John Knox, masques, music and dancing were regular entertainments. Alexander Scott and George Buchanan were employed as court poets, with a remit to script many of the court masques; also employed were female court jesters, including Mary's favourites, two Frenchwomen nicknamed La Jardinière and La Folle. For outdoor enjoyment Mary continued to ride every day and hunt whenever she could, and she also introduced to the court a competitive team game on horseback called 'running the ring'. On winter evenings, playing cards or dice or billiards were favourite pastimes.

The court setting was also magnificent. Mary made sure the interiors of her royal palaces were refurbished with rich hangings on the walls, embroidered coverings on beds and cushions on seats. She herself continued to be fashionable and sumptuous in her dress: the inventory of her clothes in 1562 listed 131 items, including sixty gowns of cloth of gold, silver, velvet, satin and silk. A dozen neck furs of ermine and sable brought from France provided much-needed warmth, as well as elegance. Mary sometimes donned Highland cloaks, and on occasion dressed up in disguise. At one banquet given for the French ambassador she and the four Maries wore men's clothing in a masque; and on Easter Monday 1565 they ran along the streets of Stirling dressed up as burgesses' wives.

Despite this life of luxury and enjoyment, Mary was still subject to bouts of illness and depression. She was badly unnerved by an incident at court in late 1562, when a young French poet, Pierre de Boscol, Seigneur de Chastelard, twice entered her bedchamber without permission; infatuated with the queen, the first time he hid under the bed and the second he made romantic advances towards her. As a result of these intrusions, she would not go to sleep for some time afterwards unless Mary Fleming stayed in the same room. She was also deeply grieved to learn, in March 1563, of the assassination of her favourite uncle, the Duke of Guise. Not long afterwards she confided to Randolph that she felt 'destitute of all friendship', and confessed that the burden of rule was almost too much to bear. During 1563 and 1564, the slow and tortuous progress of her marriage negotiations also took its toll, and Randolph reported on her 'melancholies' and tendency to weep often 'when there is little apparent occasion'.[39] After her birthday in 1564 she was ill with a pain in her right side, which Knox maliciously put down to too much dancing, but was more likely caused by a gastric ulcer. A similar stomach pain recurred throughout her life at times of nervous strain.

Soon after she had recovered from this last illness, Mary became acquainted with her future husband, her cousin Henry Stewart, Lord Darnley. Born in England in December 1545, Darnley was the son of Lady Margaret Douglas, the Countess of Lennox, and Matthew Stewart, 4th Earl of Lennox. On both sides of his family Darnley possessed royal blood. His mother was the daughter of Margaret Tudor by her second husband, while his father was the great-great-grandson of King James II of Scotland (d. 1460) and had a claim to the Scottish succession. Lennox, who had defected to the English side during the period of the 'Rough Wooing', had lived in exile in England since 1544, but in September 1564 Elizabeth allowed him to return home to Scotland as an act of goodwill towards Mary. In February 1565 Darnley followed in his wake, with permission to remain in Scotland for three months. It has sometimes been alleged that Elizabeth sent him north to trap her enemy into marrying a dissolute character, but the evidence suggests she had no such plan.

Mary and Darnley had first met in December 1560 at Orléans, where he had gone to offer the recently widowed queen the condolences of his family. At that time Darnley's mother was apparently thinking of him as a potential second husband for his cousin, but Mary displayed no interest in the fifteen-year-old boy. When they met again at the castle of Wemyss in Fife in February 1565, Mary recognized that Darnley – now a twenty-year-old man – was an eye-catching figure, telling Melville 'that he was the lustiest and best proportioned long man that she had seen'.[40] Darnley was indeed handsome, if rather effeminate, as well as slim, elegant and unusually tall. At well over six feet, he stood taller than Mary, who towered over most men. However, the queen did not single him out as a favourite nor think of marriage to him until after she had received confirmation from Elizabeth, on 15 March 1565, that a marriage to Leicester would not result in the recognition of her title to the English succession. Indeed, in this message Elizabeth went even further and announced that she would make no decision at all on the succession until she herself had either married or resolved not to do so.

On learning this, Mary 'wept her fill'[41] and totally dismissed any further consideration of the Leicester match. Instead she turned towards Darnley, marriage to whom seemed to offer both personal pleasure and political advantage. His looks were appealing and his manners charming; but, most important of all, by marrying him Mary would unite the two Stewart claimants to the English succession in one dynastic marriage, and lessen objections that as an alien she and her children could not inherit the English throne.

No sooner had Mary received Elizabeth's rebuff than it became noticeable that she and Darnley were spending more time together. On 20 March 1565 Randolph reported that the lord was much esteemed by the Scottish queen, but that a marriage between them was, in his opinion, unlikely. By mid-April Randolph had changed his mind and gave his opinion that a marriage would probably take place. In the intervening weeks Mary had evidently fallen in love with her cousin. Their intimacy had developed when, at the beginning of April, he had become seriously ill at Stirling Castle. Mary visited his bedside at all hours, lavishing care on the young man who seemed so sick and vulnerable. Little did she know that the patient was probably suffering from the early symptoms of syphilis, rather than the prolonged attack of measles that was then diagnosed. Nor did she realize that Darnley's outbursts of ill temper were typical of his unpleasant and temperamental character, rather than merely symptoms of an

invalid's fractiousness. Even before he had fully recovered, Mary had decided to marry him, and as soon as he was well enough to get up (15 May), he was knighted and created Baron Ardmannoch and Earl of Ross in preparation for his betrothal to the queen.

Elizabeth reacted to the news that Mary intended to marry her cousin with anger and dismay. Her main fear – one that was fuelled by her councillors – was that the marriage was part of a plot to depose her and restore Roman Catholicism by launching an invasion or inciting a rebellion in northern England. The Countess of Lennox was a Catholic, and although Darnley had attended Protestant services in England, he too was thought to be Catholic. To deter Mary from the marriage, Elizabeth dispatched Throckmorton to Scotland with instructions to tell the Scottish queen how much she disliked it. Mary, however, denied that Elizabeth had any reason to complain: in her view, she had tried to reach a formal amity with the English queen and it was not her fault that the negotiations had come to nothing. Furthermore, she protested, it was her right as a queen and a woman to choose her own husband. Elizabeth's response was to summon Darnley and Lennox to England, a command that Mary encouraged them both to disobey. In retaliation, and as a security measure, Elizabeth put the Countess of Lennox in the Tower and forbade her to receive any communication from her husband and son.

In Scotland the match was also unpopular in some quarters. Moray, Châtelherault and

OPPOSITE

Genealogical Chart, 1619 by Benjamin Wright after an unknown artist. This chart illustrates how both Mary and Henry Darnley (row two) descended from Henry VII and Elizabeth of York. Their son James VI of Scotland and I of England appears at the top of the chart with his wife, Anne of Denmark. (National Portrait Gallery, London)

Archibald Campbell, 5th Earl of Argyll, believed it was a threat to the Scottish Protestant Church as Darnley was (according to Moray) 'rather an enemy than a preferer' of 'Christ's true religion'.[42] Equally, these lords suspected that Darnley and his family would try to oust them from government and challenge their regional power once he became king. The Lennoxes had already begun building up an affinity in Argyll's heartland in Perthshire, while Darnley had been reported as saying that Moray's estates were 'too much'. Moray had an additional reason for objecting to Mary's choice. It would mean the end of the Anglophile foreign policy he had been promoting for the past five years. On 21 May 1565, to signal his strong disapproval, he left court.

To counter these opponents Mary did her best to win over her subjects 'by gentle letters and fair words',[43] and soon she could depend on the support of other important figures. Maitland was prepared to put his weight behind the marriage – albeit reluctantly – because he had fallen in love with Mary Fleming and would do anything she asked of him. The Countess of Lennox brought round members of the Douglas family by relinquishing her claim to the earldom of Angus, which James Douglas, the 4th Earl of Morton, was administering. Thereafter, Darnley could rely on the backing of Morton and Lords Patrick Lindsay and Patrick Ruthven whose wives were Douglases. Other noblemen who were jealous of Moray's power were pleased to see the Lennox family gain influence at the earl's expense.

In July 1565 Mary laid down the final preparations for her marriage. She was in something of a hurry for she had heard rumours of a plot to kidnap Darnley and return him to England. She therefore did not wait to receive the papal dispensation (necessary before marriage to a first cousin), which was issued only in September and backdated to 25 May. On the morning of Sunday 22 July the banns for the wedding were read, and afterwards Darnley was created Duke of Albany, a title reserved for Scottish royalty. A week later, just before sundown on the Saturday evening, Mary's heralds announced that the marriage was to be solemnized and that Darnley was to be 'King of this our kingdom'. Normally such a title required the agreement of parliament, but Mary (for once attending a meeting of the council) had persuaded sufficient of its members to approve it. According to the imperial ambassador to England, her insistence in this matter was because she had 'previously been married to one of the greatest kings in Christendom and therefore intended to wed no one unless he were a king'.[44]

On Sunday 29 July at about six in the morning Mary married Darnley, now King Henry, in the Chapel Royal at Holyrood. She was dressed in the *deuil blanc* mourning she had worn for her husband: a black gown, white hood and filmy veil to signify that she was coming to her new husband not as a virgin maid but as dowager queen of France. The Catholic ceremony was quite short, and afterwards a nuptial Mass was heard, although by arrangement Darnley did not attend it in order to avoid offending Scottish Protestants. Afterwards, Mary joined her husband in her chamber, where all those attending the wedding removed a pin from her veil, and possibly the sleeves of her mourning gown, to symbolize her departure from sorrow into a new and happy married life. She then retired with her ladies and changed into festive garments. The rest of the day passed in celebrations, until at last she and her new husband went to bed. For the next three days there were balls and entertainments.

Until she made the decision to marry Darnley, Mary had served her country and dynastic interests quite well. On the debit side, she can certainly be criticized for a lack of energy and commitment in the day-to-day running of Scotland. It is clear that she was more interested in hunting than hard work. She rarely attended council meetings, and gave no lead in suggesting legislative initiatives. This mattered in Scotland far more than it did in England because of the nature of its kingship and institutions. Consequently, as Jenny Wormald has pointed out, the amount of business carried out in council and parliament during the years 1561 to 1565 was exceptionally limited. Despite this, Mary displayed important strengths in governing Scotland. She was not wayward or untrustworthy, but ruled with counsel and consistency. By not appointing new men to power, she avoided bringing factionalism into Scottish politics. By maintaining the status quo in ecclesiastical matters, as she had promised her half-brother in France, she also avoided the upheavals of

religious strife. In continuing the amity with England, she carried out a foreign policy that satisfied the preferences of her Protestant subjects and suited her own aspirations. This policy was seen as neither weak nor dishonourable, for Mary consistently refused to ratify the Treaty of Edinburgh as it stood or to marry according to the will of Elizabeth, except on her own terms. Furthermore, Mary was a queen with charisma, whose court attracted poets, musicians and writers, and impressed foreigners and Scots, though not, of course, preachers such as Knox. Although too often ill and tearful to be truly authoritative, Mary did present an image of majesty that dazzled many men – even those who were unsympathetic to her religion.

Overall, therefore, during her personal rule, Mary showed a good grasp of political realities and performed the role of queen with some aplomb. But her success in these years owed much to the good advice offered by her experienced and politically astute ministers, Moray and Maitland, and sensibly taken by the queen. With her marriage to Darnley, Moray disappeared from her council, and Maitland was marginalized. The result was disastrous.

STVART·

CHAPTER FOUR
Married Queen of Scotland
1565–1567

B OTH DARNLEY AND MARY were determined that they should rule jointly. Darnley was equally determined, and Mary at least compliant, that he as the man should take precedence over his wife, even though she was the hereditary sovereign. Consequently, the inscription on the silver coin minted to commemorate their marriage referred to 'Henricus et Maria D. Gra. R & R. Scotorum' (Henry and Mary by Grace of God King and Queen of Scotland). Similarly, when proclaiming King Henry for a second time on the day after the wedding, the heralds gave Henry precedence over Mary. The nobles who heard this announcement were stunned, and only one voice – that of the Earl of Lennox, Darnley's father – shouted out 'God save his Grace'. Henry, however, was not satisfied with the title of king. He thirsted after the crown matrimonial, which had been granted to Mary's first husband, for this would allow him to exercise authority in his own right and permit him to continue ruling if his wife died childless. Mary, however, had no power to grant the crown without the consent of parliament. As time went by, moreover, she had second thoughts herself about the wisdom of conferring such authority on Henry. As a result, the crown matrimonial came to be a major bone of contention between husband and wife.

OPPOSITE
Portrait of Mary Queen of Scots, c.1569. This portrait was painted around the time of Mary's marriage to Darnley. (The Blairs Museum, Aberdeen)

ABOVE

Silver ryal issued in honour of Mary's marriage to Darnley (1565). Henry is given precedence over Mary on this coin, both in the inscription ('Henry and Mary by the Grace of God King and Queen of Scotland'), and in being on the left, the place traditionally reserved for the hereditary monarch in a double-portrait. (British Museum)

OPPOSITE

Letter from Mary to an unknown Scottish Protestant lord, dated 16 July 1565. It is in the hand of one of Mary's secretaries, who uses the Scottish form of spelling. In this missive Mary tries to rally support against her half-brother Moray, who was planning rebellion. She denies the 'evil bruit and untrue report spread by seditious persons amongst our Lords [lieges]' that she intended 'to impede or molest any [of] our subjects in the using of their religion and conscience freely'. She had already written a general denial, but she is now writing this personal letter 'to certify and assure you' that she will never molest him or any other in the use of their religion. Mary proved successful in isolating Moray and detaching him from most of the Protestant lords. (British Library, Cotton Caligula B X, vol. 2, f. 327)

Moray did not become reconciled to the marriage. He had withdrawn from court in May 1565, and did not reappear when summoned before Mary to explain his conduct. Believing with good cause that he planned outright rebellion, Mary took swift action to build up her support and isolate her half-brother. She bestowed royal patronage lavishly, raising, for example, Lord John Erskine to the earldom of Mar. Ten days before her wedding she recalled James Hepburn, 4th Earl of Bothwell (Moray's deadly enemy) from France, and a few days after the wedding she restored Huntly's son (Moray's rival in the north) to his father's title and lands. She and Henry also did their best to allay fears about religion in order to separate Moray from his erstwhile Protestant allies and expose the hollowness of his charge that the Darnley marriage threatened the existing religious settlement. Before their wedding Henry attended services at St Giles and heard Knox preach, while Mary ate meat at Lent for the first time and in June attended her first Protestant service.

On 6 August 1565 Mary felt strong enough to declare Moray an outlaw ('put to the horn' as it was called) and warned Châtelherault and Argyll that they, too, would be outlawed unless they deserted him. On 14 August the properties of the rebels were confiscated, and the following week Mary began raising an army. She then reissued the proclamation of August 1561, which had promised to make no change to religion. On 26 August she and her husband rode out from Edinburgh at the head of eight to

Traist freind We greit zow weill. The evill bruite and untrew report spred be seditious personis amangis oure liegis hes grebit Not in deid ... that We suld have intentit to impede or molest ony oure subiectis in ye using of thair religioun and conscience ... a thing quhilk never enterit in oure mynde Albeit ... mony ... credeit the report And to ye effect that this ... bruite may be dampnit as a thing without ground or occasioun We have diriect ... leis to signifie oure sincere meaning to all oure gud subiectis And ... that We tho it bene meite and convenient to wryt unto zow in perticular as ane of quhome We never had bot gud opinion and ... ze reddy gud will to ... quhen ye occasioun of ye commoun Weill requireit. The effect is to certifie and assure zow that as hidder tillis ze have never persavit ... ony stop stay or molestatioun to zow or ony utheris in using zour religioun and conscience ... so may ze luke for ye same ... gude will and ... in tyme cuming ... meit gud behaving zow as a gude subiect to Not Think na uther bot to find Not a favorabill and beneficiall Maisteris and prince willing to defend zow in gude ... and quietnes but Innovatioun or alteratioun in ony sorte And ... ze sall desist to ... with ony man as under pretens of the ... bruite / We pray zow to stay and tak na heide to ... that sa sall desire zow as alstra ... ... We to do ... With oure auld ... or utherways We luke to be certifeit be zow ... in Weill ... ye ... quhat We may happin for ... zow ... farther of oure mynd We have declarit to ye berar heirof _____ quhome ze sall gyf firme credite Subscrivit With oure hand At Edinburgh the ... day of Julij 1565

Efter this ... leis written ... We ... that ... ... We to have ... We ar ... ... that ze ... ... ze ma mak this ... him to Not and ... ... Not ... the ... efter ... to ... and ... zow Not ... ... him ... or ... ... ze may luke ... me ... ... that We luke to ... ... We ... not ... ze will ... ... to oure ... ... We ... ...

MARIE R

...

Double-portrait of Mary Queen of Scots and Her Husband, Lord Darnley, c.1565. In this portrait Mary and Henry are shown to be of equal height and status, but Henry is again on the left, Mary's rightful place as hereditary monarch. Although the couple ruled together after their marriage, they soon began quarrelling. (National Trust, Hardwick Hall)

ten thousand men to pursue Moray and Châtelherault in the direction of Ayr where they had last been seen. Wearing a steel cap on her head and with a pistol in her saddle holster, Mary fashioned herself as a warrior queen. John Stewart, 4th Earl of Atholl, meanwhile, was sent to the Highlands to deal with Argyll.

Moray and Châtelherault wanted to avoid a military engagement since they were greatly outnumbered, and they therefore turned away from Ayrshire and advanced on the capital with their men. There they were subjected to a heavy artillery bombardment launched by the keeper of the castle, the newly created Earl of Mar. Consequently, they withdrew to Dumfries, fifty miles to the south-west, where they waited in vain for reinforcements from Elizabeth I. The king and queen, meanwhile, re-entered Edinburgh and quickly took action to prevent defections to the rebels; those who had already joined Moray were fined or banished, and a bond of obedience was imposed on the greater part of the nobility and gentlemen of Fife (Moray's heartland). In early October 1565 Mary felt strong enough to move against Moray, and she and Henry set out at the head of a royal army towards Dumfries. Moray and his allies, however, were in no position to fight without English military and financial support, and they fled over the border, seeking asylum and aid from Elizabeth. They were to be disappointed: although she offered Moray protection and tried to secure pardons for the rebels, she publicly upbraided the earl for his disobedience towards his legal sovereign and attempted to distance herself from his rebellion.

Mary's victory in the 'Chase-about Raid', as the abortive rebellion was aptly called, was the result of her prompt political and military action. She had successfully built up a broad coalition of Protestant and Catholic nobles against Moray, Châtelherault and Argyll by appealing to their loyalty to the Crown and presenting the rebels as fighting out of selfish not religious motives. She had raised troops swiftly and placed herself at their head. This decisive and bold response contrasts starkly with that of her rival, Elizabeth. Torn between her dislike of rebellion and fear of the Darnley marriage, Elizabeth had hesitated when Moray approached her for aid. Had she made it absolutely clear that no English military help would be forthcoming, Moray might not have rebelled; had she given him assistance, he might have been successful.

By the end of 1565 Mary was at the height of her powers. She was free from the tutelage of Moray, who was banished from Scotland. Châtelherault, who had long been a disaffected presence, went into exile in France after receiving a pardon. The alliance between England and the Scottish Protestant lords had been broken, and Elizabeth no longer possessed any influence in Scottish political life. Mary looked set to rule independently over a faction-free nobility. Furthermore, by December she was known to be pregnant. The birth of an heir could only strengthen her position in Scotland and improve her chances to be the heir to Elizabeth. Hubris, however, set in. Mary overplayed her hand, while Henry no longer held in check his ambitions or controlled his debauchery. Consequently, Mary fell out with both her husband and many of her supporters.

During the Chase-about Raid, Mary and Henry had their first publicized row. Henry wanted to appoint his father lieutenant-general of the army, whereas Mary preferred Bothwell to hold supreme command 'by reason he bears evil will against the Earl of Moray and he has promised to have him die'.[45] On this occasion Mary gave way. By November 1565 they were quarrelling again, this time over Mary's distribution of pardons; Henry was particularly angry when Mary pardoned Châtelherault and his Hamilton kin, who were old rivals of the Lennox family. At the same time, more serious disputes arose over Henry's use of the royal prerogative. Mary had expected her husband to work as her partner in governing Scotland, and soon took exception when he signed papers without her knowledge, or carried out his own separate diplomacy, or was not present when she needed him. To curb his independence Mary handed over his seal to her confidential secretary, David Rizzio, who stamped documents on his behalf. On state letters, moreover, Mary's name began to precede her husband's, thereby reversing the order that had been common before November 1565. Henry was clearly very angry about the change in his position, and began to absent himself from court. He still aimed at acquiring the crown matrimonial, but any hopes he might have entertained of receiving it were shattered on 10 February 1566, when Mary denied him the royal arms on his investiture with the French chivalric Order of St Michael.

Henry's frequent drunken and offensive behaviour also did not help their relationship; nor did Mary's refusal to share his bed, and her increasing intimacy with the Italian-born David Rizzio. Rizzio, who had begun life at court as a musician and bass singer, had been promoted to be her secretary for French affairs at the end of 1564. As her relations with her husband deteriorated, Mary would sit up late at night, making music or playing cards with her secretary. Although Henry himself had once been close to Rizzio, he now grew jealous of him and came to believe false insinuations that Mary had taken her secretary as a lover.

Perhaps the breakdown in her marriage would not have had such dire political consequences had not Mary also alienated other significant political figures, most notably Maitland, Morton, Ruthven and Lindsay. These men held several grievances against the queen. First, they disliked her reliance on her household servants for advice, and resented in particular the upstart foreigner Rizzio, who lorded over them so ostentatiously. He was blamed for the sidelining of Morton (Mary's chancellor) and Maitland (her secretary of state), and was also rumoured to be a papal agent encouraging the queen to overturn the Protestant settlement in Scotland.

Second, these lords disapproved of Mary's steadfast refusal to pardon and rehabilitate Moray. As far as the queen was concerned, her half-brother was a traitor who had betrayed his familial ties and oath of allegiance to his sovereign, and she refused to listen to pleas

The Murder of David Rizzio

Portrait of David Rizzio, late seventeenth or early eighteenth century by an unknown artist. Originally a court musician, Rizzio became Mary's confidential secretary until his murder in March 1565.
(British Museum)

Engraving of the Murder of Rizzio, frontispiece to *Life and History of Mary Queen of Scots*, Edinburgh, 1850(?). The murder took place in March 1566, during a private supper hosted by Mary in Holyrood Palace. Rizzio is shown clutching Mary's skirt while being dragged away by the assassins. Darnley seeks to restrain his wife. The story of Mary Queen of Scots became a popular subject for historians and novelists during the late eighteenth and nineteenth centuries.
(British Library, Ch 810/169)

Portrait of James Douglas, 4th Earl of Morton, 1580, attr. Arnold von Bronckhorst. Douglas was Mary's chancellor, who participated in the murder of Rizzio. After Mary's recovery of power he escaped to England, but was pardoned in December 1566. He was almost certainly one of the conspirators in the plot to murder Darnley, and later took up arms against Mary and Bothwell. This portrait was painted shortly before his execution for complicity in Darnley's murder.
(Private collection/Bridgeman Art Library)

SICKAR

JAMES DOUGLAS. E: of MORTON. REGENT.

for mercy on his behalf. Maitland, however, considered his old ally Moray had been treated too harshly, and wanted to see him readmitted to the queen's counsels, where he could speak up for the Anglophile policies that Mary now seemed to be abandoning. Even lords less sympathetic to the earl and his policies disliked Mary's intransigence towards him. Her plan to attaint Moray in parliament (which involved pronouncing him a traitor and legally confiscating his lands) made them uneasy. Taken with the treatment of Huntly in 1562, Moray's attainder could be construed as a move to assert royal power at the expense of the nobility.

Third, the Protestant lords were alarmed by what seemed to be a new direction in Mary's religious policy. She was surrounding herself with more Catholics than before, and pushing forward the interests of the Roman Church. In September 1565 the queen and king issued a proclamation intimating that at the next parliament they would introduce a statute permitting freedom of conscience. At the religious festival of Candlemas on 2 February 1566, they insisted that the leading nobles attend High Mass in the Chapel Royal. Although the Protestants amongst them refused, some three hundred people attended the ceremony – a throng that barely complied with the original agreement that Mary be allowed a private Mass just for her household. A little later Henry and his entourage strutted down the streets of Edinburgh, boasting that they would restore the Mass to the whole realm. At the same time Mary declared

ominously that she would have 'all men live as they list'[46] and be free to hear the Mass. This approach contrasted dramatically with her behaviour over the previous spring, when she had been neglecting her religious duties and encouraging her Protestant subjects to hope for her conversion.

What caused Mary's turnabout in religion? Most probably her easy defeat of Moray and the loyalty of many Protestants led her to become overconfident. Mistakenly, she believed that the time was opportune to push through a policy of toleration for her co-religionists. Away from Moray's influence, and surrounded by Catholics in her household, she simply could not see the dangers of pursuing such a policy. Perhaps, too, Mary's pregnancy led her to believe that she was now in a strong position to challenge the unmarried Elizabeth for the throne of England by playing the Catholic card. Her talks with French and papal envoys, who arrived at her court in early 1566, may have encouraged her to think that her Guise family and the pope would support her in this endeavour, provided that she was more aggressively Catholic. Certainly, in early February 1566 she declared that she was the rightful Queen of England. Whatever the cause of her shift, the result was damaging: many Protestants grew apprehensive that she intended to permit the Mass outside her chapel, and perhaps even change the established religion.

Mary had thus become isolated from both the Lennox family and the Protestant Anglophile nobles, who together began to plot against her. The facts surrounding their conspiracy are murky, since those involved later tried to escape full responsibility. Nonetheless, it does seem that Mary's chancellor, Morton, and possibly her secretary, Maitland, brokered a deal in February 1566 between the king, Argyll and Moray, whereby Henry promised to pardon the rebel leaders, prevent the forfeiture of their lands and protect the Protestant religion in return for receiving the crown matrimonial. Additionally, they all agreed that Rizzio and Mary's other foreign friends were to be ousted from power and, if necessary, murdered. This coup was to be mounted before the next parliament could pass an Act of Attainder against Moray. Who decided exactly how the seizure of power was to be carried out we do not know, but, according to Ruthven, Henry had insisted that Rizzio should be murdered in the presence of Mary. Mary was warned of the danger, but imprudently chose to brush it aside. In England Cecil and Leicester were kept well briefed of the plan, but cheerfully did nothing to forestall it since it was in England's interests to have Moray restored to power.

On Thursday 7 March 1566 Mary opened parliament in Edinburgh, and on the following Saturday evening she hosted a private supper party attended by Rizzio, the Countess of Argyll and other members of the court in a small room next to her bedchamber at Holyrood. In the middle of the meal her husband unexpectedly arrived, either to distract her attention or to witness the ensuing events.

Suddenly Ruthven, clad in full armour, burst into the room and demanded that Rizzio leave with him. Mary ordered the lord to depart, but could do nothing to protect her favourite when about eighty armed men, led by Morton and Lindsay, rushed in to take him out. Rizzio crouched helplessly behind his mistress, but one conspirator struck at him with a dagger over her shoulder. While cocked pistols were pressed into Mary's body, Rizzio was dragged away. He was found later in the porter's lodge, with at least fifty-three stab wounds in his body. The king's dagger had been left in his corpse to signal his responsibility for the deed.

Although Holyrood was surrounded by some five hundred men, Huntly, Bothwell and Atholl, who were lodging elsewhere in the palace that evening, managed to get away. Detained in captivity and threatened with death if she communicated with anyone outside, Mary did not collapse, but resourcefully planned her own escape. Despite the horrors of Rizzio's death, and fear for her own life, she kept calm and smuggled out a letter to Huntly by way of his mother. She then worked on her husband to betray his fellow conspirators. Besides inviting him to sleep with her (which in a drunken stupor he failed to take up), she warned him 'how miserably he would be handled'[47] by the Protestant lords, and how much he would be despised by his Catholic friends if he altered his religion. Won over by her arguments or the power of her personality, Henry agreed to join her in flight. In the early hours of 12 March 1566 they both slipped out of the palace, with

Right trusty and welbeloved Cousingis We greit you hertely
weill. Insafar as We have understand be report of ...
... Robert McCuile the gude effect maid to our behuif be the
Q. our gude Sister your Soverane ... tyme our self ...
quhatsoever a gude Sister and tender cousing mycht quhen she ...
... And that we culd not declair the affe...
we bear toward our said Dearest Sister bettir nor be that quhilk
did quhen we ... not believe brocht this ...
... that seruid ... gude tyme our meaning we ... that the
cair of the prottectioun of our ... sum seik rest upoun our said gude ...
We beleve ye have alwayes bene gude ministeris to mak ...
to schaw hir allin reasonable favor to our advancement in that ...
... and from the Lordis ye will ... gentilness. We tak ...
self (as we doubt not but ye knaw) to be the Q. our Soverane ...
... cousing and most gracious and the lauchfull ... of the
body to have grittest interest of all other to that quhilk ...
(as is reportit) Laitlie mentionat in the parliament hous ...
albeit we be not of mynd to press our said gude Sister furthir
then sall cum of hir allin gude plesir we put that matter in ...
That becaus in that caus we wald mycht be the Lawis of the realme
of England, we do effectuuslie require you, to have respect to me ...
with indifferency quhensoever it sall pleis the Q. our Soverane to ...
the same matter in deliberatioun. And to the we we will na ...
insist thairin but sik tyme as it sall pleis hir self to ... we ...
Mawnyng. We desyr you in the meyntyme to have that opinioun ...
we, that as we mynd to gritness all our lyff in gude intelli...
with the Q. our Soverane and that realme Sa gif ony ...
wald offend the same we wald withstand hym at our ... pow...
and that ye can not advise our said Dearest Sister to extend hir ...
beharit ony that sall requyre it in a bettir sort. And sa ...
commit you to the prottectioun of god at Dumbar the ... of ...
Day of November 1568

Your gude Consignani

Mary's Illness: November 1566

OPPOSITE

Letter from Mary to the lords of Elizabeth's council, dated 18 November 1566. In this letter Mary is seeking to create a new amity with England, based on a strong personal relationship with Elizabeth. When, earlier that month, Mary was seriously ill, she placed her son under the 'special care of the protection' of Elizabeth. Although now recovered, Mary renews that pledge in this letter to Elizabeth's councillors. She then asks them to behave justly and impartially when Elizabeth makes a decision on the succession, as she has just been petitioned to do by parliament. Mary knew very well that Elizabeth's councillors were suspicious of her and generally hostile to her claim to be heir to the throne (thirteen lines down):

'We take ourself (as we doubt not but you knoweth) to be the Q[ueen] your sovereign's next cousin and next herself and the lawful issue of her body, to have greatest interest of all other to that which has been (as is reported) lately motioned in the Parliament-House; and albeit we be not of mind to prise our good sister further than shall come of her own good pleasure till put that matter in question, yet because in that case we will be judged by the laws of the realm of England, we do effectuously require you to have respect of justice with indifferency, whensoever it shall please the Q[ueen] your sovereign to put the same matter in deliberation. And to us we will no wise insist therein unto such time as it shall please herself to give us warning.'

In the margin an English clerk has summarized the letter's contents.

(British Library, Cotton Caligula B X, f. 403)

ABOVE

Craigmillar Castle. During the autumn of 1566 Mary suffered from ill health. While at Craigmillar Castle in November, she underwent a complete physical and emotional collapse. Once she had recovered, her councillors discussed with her the problem of her husband. They certainly raised the question of divorce, and may also have hinted at the desirability of an assassination.

(British Library, 010028.de.1/1)

assistance from the captain of her guard and a few other trusted servants, and made for Dunbar Castle, where Bothwell and Huntly were based. Although six months pregnant, Mary coped with a gruelling five-hour journey on horseback, pushed to the limits by an unsympathetic husband who was even more scared about capture than she was. At Dunbar loyal supporters gathered around. With their help she raised a substantial army, and on 18 March rode back into Edinburgh. Once there, she chose not to return to Holyrood, which was poorly defended, but took up residence in the stronghold of Edinburgh Castle to await her confinement.

Mary's main priority, before the birth of her child, was to reconcile her factious lords and bring those who were not directly responsible for Rizzio's murder into government. She therefore pardoned Moray (who had wisely arrived at Holyrood the night after the murder) and Argyll (who did not arrive until two weeks later), and by the end of April both men were restored to the council. But no clemency was shown to Rizzio's actual murderers. Morton, Lindsay, Ruthven and the rest escaped to England, where Ruthven died three months later. Knox, who had expressed approval of the murder, fled to Ayrshire, while Maitland, against whom nothing could be proved, left court of his own accord until September 1566, when he again attended council meetings through the mediation of Moray.

Henry brazenly protested total innocence in Rizzio's murder, and for a time Mary was prepared to believe his denials. But his co-conspirators sent Mary the bond he had signed, committing him to the assassination, and from then on she loathed and distrusted her husband. She also suspected that he had organized the murder to take place in her presence so that she would miscarry and possibly die. She needed, however, to make it appear that nothing was amiss in their relationship because the legitimacy of her unborn child had to be beyond dispute. Consequently, Henry's name continued to appear on state papers, and on Maundy Thursday they carried out together the ritual of washing the feet of the poor. There was no talk of separation.

On Wednesday 19 June 1566, Mary gave birth to a healthy boy. There was great rejoicing in Edinburgh, and Sir James Melville was immediately dispatched to relay the good news to Elizabeth in England. According to Melville's oft-quoted memoirs, written some time afterwards and not entirely trustworthy, the English queen's first reaction was gloom: 'all merriness was laid aside for the night', he wrote, and she burst out to some of her ladies 'that the Queen of Scots was lighter of a fair son, while she was but a barren stock'.[48] With a male heir now secured in Scotland, Melville decided that the time was opportune to broach the succession issue once more, and, somewhat to his surprise, Elizabeth answered in a positive vein. Melville was told 'that the birth of the prince was to her a great spur to cause the most skilful lawyers in England to use greater diligence in trying out that matter, which she esteemed to belong most justly to her good sister'. Furthermore, Melville noticed that Leicester, Norfolk, Pembroke and several other English lords 'showed themselves more openly her [Mary's] friend' when they heard the news of the prince's birth.[49]

The birth of the prince, however, did nothing to repair his parents' marriage. After her confinement Mary neither slept nor ate with Henry, and their quarrels became more bitter and abusive; in one row Mary, it was said, used words that 'cannot for modesty nor with the honour of a queen be reported'.[50] On the one side, Mary treated her husband with suspicion and disdain; on the other, Henry resented her suspicions and was jealous of her relationships with other people, men and women alike. Far from seeking to appease her and build up trust, he continued to scheme with Catholics in England, and also wrote to the pope and kings of France and Spain, accusing his wife of failing in her duty to restore Catholicism. Knowing this, Mary feared that he intended to seize the crown for himself. Matters came to a head when, on 29 September 1566, she learnt from her father-in-law that Henry planned to leave the realm because he was so humiliated by her refusal to give him the crown matrimonial. His departure would not only be a public insult, but also a political threat, so she tackled him about this information privately. Henry, however, gave no satisfactory answer. The following day she raised the matter again, this time in front of her councillors and the French ambassador. Henry again produced no explanation, but

disrespectfully departed without bowing to the queen, simply uttering the words, 'Adieu Madam, you shall not see my face for a long space'.[51] In fact, Mary saw him just a week later, when he again behaved unreasonably towards her, but from then on they lived mostly apart.

Soon afterwards, on 7 October 1566, Mary visited the borders to hold her courts of justice. While at Jedburgh, she learnt that Bothwell, her lieutenant of the borders, had been ambushed and badly wounded. Consequently, after conducting the Justice Ayre, which took about a week, she rode on horseback to visit him. Later on, her enemies claimed that this visit to Bothwell's castle at Hermitage proved 'her outrageous lust' for the earl and her adultery,[52] but the allegation is absurd. Mary visited Bothwell because he was her trusted official and councillor; she waited a week before setting out to see him; and she stayed with him for only a couple of hours, and always in the company of Moray and other courtiers.

One or two days after this ride, Mary became seriously sick and almost died. She was in agony from pain in her side, vomited blood, and suffered convulsions. Her symptoms indicate she was suffering from a perforated gastric ulcer, brought on by intense physical exercise and emotional strain. During her illness Henry made but one brief appearance at her bedside, and then went off hunting. 'This is such a fault,' wrote the French ambassador, 'as I know not how to apologize

Instruccions given to the Erle of Bedford one
of the Lordes of her Ma.ts privie Counsell,
Lord Warden of the estmarchees towardes
Scotland and Governor of the Towne of
Barwick sent by the Q. Ma.tie into Scotland
to be an assistant at the Christeninge of the
Q. of Scotts Sonne ye prince there.

7° Novembr: 1566.

The first cause of yor sendinge is this, Wheras the Q. of Scotts
hath required us to be godmother to her sonne as she
hath in like manner required the french, Kinge and the
Duke of Savoy to be godfathers, on whose behalf certen
persons of honor and degree are appointed by the said
kinge and duke. Whereof for the french kinge
the Comte of Brienne is allreadie come, and as we
heare the Marquesse of Chamberry shall come
for the duke. We doe therfor thought meete to direct
yow on our behalf to repaire to our said Sister the
Quene first to declare to her that according to our
former agreement upon the first sendinge hither we have
sent yow to assist and attend upon such, a person that in
her Realme as not shold make choise to supplie our
place with is our dere and welbeloved Cosin the
Countesse of Argile, whome we are bold with the
leave of our good Sister to appoint and require therto
because we could not towardes this winter tyme send
any Ladie of our own Realme with suertie of their
safe passage in so longe and hard a jorney for Ladies
to travell in, And beside that we have the rather made
choise of her for her nearenes in bloud and welbeloved a
Sister she is to the Quene our good Sister. And
accordinge herunto yow shall also afterward deliver
our lre to the said Countesse, with our most hartie re-
commendacions and our earnest requst to take the paines
to supplie our place, with suertie with all our hart we
would as gladlie doe our selves as she shall if so commoditie and conveniencie might aswell suffer it as our
desire would further yt. As for the Manner of yor
attendance and assistaunce at this Christeninge yow shall
followe suche directions or orders there as yow shall see
most honorable for us and gratefull to our good Sister
And for avoydinge of suche matters as might be harmfull
to yor Conscience and sclaunderous in example to our
profession in Religion, we thinke it good that therein
yow doe forbeare in such sort as yow shall perceave the
Erle of Murray or such of his sort doe by ye permission
of the Quene their Soveraigne. And yow shall
also present unto our Sister the ffront of gold at
such convenient tyme as yow may see at the tyme
of the makinge of it now this somer that ymmediatly
upon knowledge of the birth of her sonne was
mette for her Comte then now we thinke it is by
reason of this growinge and therefore sure yt may be

A Royal Christening

Instructions from Elizabeth to the Earl of Bedford, 7 November 1566, regarding the christening of Mary's son on 17 December. Elizabeth sent six pages of instructions to Bedford, who was dispatched to Scotland to attend the ceremony. In them she explains that Mary has asked her to be godmother, and the French king and Duke of Savoy to be godfathers, and that they are sending representatives (see twelve lines down):

'...we have sent you to assist and attend upon such a person there in her realm, as we have made choice to supply our place, which is our dear and well-beloved cousin, the Countess of Argyll.' Elizabeth tells Bedford that he should avoid participating in ceremonies 'as might be harmful to your conscience and slanderous in example to our profession in religion', and she goes on to say that it would therefore be good for him to follow the example of Murray (Moray) as to whether or not to attend the religious services. Elizabeth also instructs Bedford to present Mary with her present of 'the font of gold'.
(British Library, Cotton Caligula B X, f. 399)

Portrait of Francis Russell, 2nd Earl of Bedford, c.1780. Bedford was sworn into Elizabeth's Privy Council in 1558, and used on diplomatic missions to France and Scotland. Appointed Governor of Berwick and Lord Warden of the Eastern March in 1564, he had an interest in Scottish affairs. He was sent as Elizabeth's representative to the christening of Mary's son.
(British Library, C.6.e.7)

for it.'[53] On 9 November Mary was well enough to go on royal progress through East Lothian and Berwickshire, but while at Craigmillar Castle just outside Edinburgh she collapsed again. This time her symptoms were less physical than emotional; according to one eyewitness, she was afflicted with 'a deep grief and sorrow' and repeated the words 'I could wish to be dead'.[54] In this state of depression, Mary gave serious thought to her own mortality. She had made a will before her confinement, but now she was more concerned about the future of her child than the disposal of her possessions. Consequently, she sent a message to Elizabeth, asking her to take up 'the special care of the protection of our son'. In this way, Mary hoped, he would be protected from the ambitions of his father and in a strong position to inherit the throne of England.

Mary's relationship with her husband troubled her councillors as well as the queen. They despised Henry for his betrayal in March 1566, blamed him for the breakdown in Mary's health, and feared his intrigues with the Catholic European powers. While at Craigmillar, five of Mary's principal councillors (Moray, Maitland, Bothwell, Huntly and Argyll) discussed together how best to be rid of him, and on 20 November they approached Mary with their suggestions. No records were kept of the meetings, and historians give different accounts of them based on later testimonies and their own suppositions. Unquestionably, Maitland proposed an annulment or divorce, and Mary agreed, provided it would be 'not

prejudicial to her son' by raising questions about his legitimacy. Probably, Maitland also hinted at other ways Mary might 'be quit of' Henry, for she reportedly told the lords: 'I will that ye do nothing whereto any spot may be laid to my honour or conscience, and therefore I pray you rather let the matter be in the estate as it is.'[55] It is by no means clear, however, exactly what Maitland was proposing. Huntly, Argyll and Maitland afterwards professed that they were thinking of convicting Henry of treason in parliament, but others (who were not at Craigmillar) claimed that the lords were in fact proposing his murder. Whether true or not, Mary's words imply that she rejected any such course of action if it were indeed put before her.

Meanwhile, during late November and early December 1566, Mary's thoughts focused on her son's baptism. She planned a grand three-day event, one that would celebrate not only the birth of a prince of Scotland, but also a future king of England. At the same time she intended to broadcast the authority of her regime and the political reconciliation she had achieved since March. The occasion was so important to her that to pay for it she raised direct taxation from her subjects (the only time in her reign) and borrowed £12,000 from Edinburgh merchants. The baptism itself took place in the late afternoon of Tuesday 17 December 1566 in the Chapel Royal at Stirling. The boy was named Charles James, the first name (which was not used) to honour his godfather, the King of France, and in memory of Charlemagne. Elizabeth was the godmother, but as the service was performed according to Catholic rites, her special ambassador, Francis Russell, the 2nd Earl of Bedford, did not attend, although the Protestant Countess of Argyll participated as her proxy.

Like Bedford, the Scottish Protestant lords stood outside the chapel during the religious service, but they fully participated in the celebrations afterwards. Indeed, at the formal dinner the earls of Bothwell, Moray and Huntly, once such bitter enemies, all played an equally prominent role in the proceedings in order to signify to the outside world their reconciliation. Reconciliation was also the main theme of the triumphs, entertainments and masques of the next few days, modelled as they were on festivities that had been staged in France the previous year to signify the end of religious turmoil. At the same time, imagery was used that was associated with the mythical English king, Arthur, who had been appropriated by the Tudors as their direct ancestor, with a strong emphasis on Merlin's prophesy, which looked to the union of Britain. The only sour note in the festivities was the absence of the baby's father, who sulkily kept to his own apartments at Stirling.

Once the baptism was over, Mary concentrated on rebuilding her friendship with Elizabeth. The portents were good, as Elizabeth had instructed Bedford (sent to Scotland for the baptism) to begin the process of re-establishing the 'amity' between the two monarchs. Elizabeth would do her part by allowing the 1560 Treaty of Edinburgh to be

renegotiated, as Mary had asked five years earlier. Furthermore, although Elizabeth still dismissed any idea of parliamentary recognition of Mary's title, she promised that 'we will never do or suffer any thing that may be to the prejudice of her title, and shall declare against any who shall invade the same'.[56] To demonstrate her own good will Mary reluctantly agreed, on Christmas Eve 1566, to heed Bedford's fervent pleas that she put aside her personal feelings and grant a pardon to Morton and the other murderers of Rizzio. She did, however, forbid them to come within seven miles of the court for two years. Early in the New Year Mary wrote to thank Elizabeth for these signs of friendship and to tell her she would send some of her council to treat with her.

Morton's return destabilized the fragile peace that had operated in Scotland during his exile, for the earl was determined on revenge for Henry's treachery in the Rizzio plot. On 18 or 19 January 1567 Morton met Maitland, Bothwell and Archibald Douglas (his cousin and Bothwell's brother-in-law) at Whittingham Castle in East Lothian, where they discussed and planned Henry's murder. Moray may have been told of the plot, but this cannot be proved, and, as to be expected, he strongly denied involvement afterwards. There is no evidence at all that Mary approved the scheme, despite the accusations that sprang up later. The 'Casket Letters' that were to be used as proof of her guilt cannot be trusted, since some were forgeries, others doctored originals and the rest inconclusive. Undoubtedly, though, Mary had some inkling that her

Diagram of the murder of Darnley at Kirk o' Field, February 1567, drawn for Cecil shortly after Darnley's lodgings were blown up. The corpses of Darnley and his servant were found in a garden some forty feet away, as seen on the top right. Darnley is wearing his nightgown, and near him are placed a doublet, chair, dagger and rope. In the top left his son James, sitting up in bed, is crying out for vengeance. (National Archives, Kew)

husband was in danger. Rumours of a threat to his life were circulating in Scotland in January, and Mary could hardly have been ignorant of them. Furthermore, in a story, which Mary did not deny, Archibald Douglas later claimed that he had asked Mary to authorize the killing, which she refused to do.

Mary was, therefore, not directly implicated in the plot against Henry, but it seems likely that she knew his days were numbered and was content to leave him to his fate. After all, an assassination carried out by his personal enemies would certainly have solved her marital and political problems. Henry was not only an embarrassment, but also dangerous, for he was known to be plotting against her and her son. Other ways of dealing with him were problematic: a divorce might well impugn the legitimacy of the prince, while putting Henry on trial for treason would create legal difficulties and cause a protracted international scandal. It is true that Mary had to avoid any dishonour, especially now that her diplomacy with Elizabeth was reaching fruition, but if Morton and the Douglases, who had a blood feud with Henry, acted independently, why should she be held responsible?

In early January 1567 Henry was safe, lying ill in the Lennox stronghold of Glasgow. On learning that his enemies had been pardoned, he had understandably felt insecure at Stirling Castle and departed on Christmas Eve for Glasgow, with the intention of going abroad shortly afterwards. On his journey, however, he

had been struck down with a fever and an eruption of livid pustules over his whole body, which was probably a recurrence of the symptoms of syphilis. Mary set out to see him, arriving at Glasgow on Wednesday 22 January. According to her own account, written while in captivity in England, she was merely responding to his messages asking for a visit, but most historians believe she went with the intention of transporting him back to Edinburgh or its vicinity. Why did she want the move? Her detractors have claimed that she needed Henry to be in an unfortified building that his murderers could easily enter, but this explanation is unconvincing because Mary had arranged for the patient to stay at Craigmillar Castle and not the undefended house in Kirk o' Field. It was Darnley who rejected the original location, because he wished to be close to his wife. Her defenders, meanwhile, have contended that her motives were completely innocent. One historian has argued that on seeing Henry so helpless and repentant, she felt pity towards him and decided to patch up their marriage, but this is barely credible. Others maintain that she still loathed and distrusted her husband, and her intention was to keep him under her surveillance away from his Lennox supporters, in order to stop him plotting against her and her son. This explanation seems by far the most likely.

Henry was reluctant to leave Glasgow, but Mary persuaded him to go with her by promising a full reconciliation, which he took to mean a resumption of sexual relations and his return to political influence. The couple arrived in Edinburgh at the beginning of February. He took up temporary residence in the Old Provost's Lodging at Kirk o' Field (named after the Church of St Mary in the Field), just inside the town wall, in what was regarded as the healthy part of the town. Mary intended him to remain there until his face had recovered from its blisters and he was thought unlikely to infect their son. Mary continued to live at Holyrood, but visited Henry several times, and on two occasions stayed overnight in a separate downstairs room. According to a letter written by Henry to his father, Mary had behaved throughout his convalescence 'like a natural and loving wife'.[57] On the evening of Sunday 9 February she called on him in the evening with a party of nobles, including Argyll, Bothwell and Huntly. It was the last Sunday of Lent, and Mary had spent the day at a wedding for two of her servants and a farewell banquet for the Savoyard ambassador. Some time around 11.00 p.m. she and the nobles left to attend the wedding masque at Holyrood, much to the annoyance of Henry, who had hoped she would stay the night. By then he was fully recovered, and planned to move to Holyrood the next day.

A little after 2.00 a.m. the people of Edinburgh heard a loud explosion. The Old Provost's Lodging had been blown up and was in ruins. A few hours later the corpses of Henry and his valet, both clad in their nightgowns, were found in a nearby garden on the other side of the town wall. Near them

lay a belt with a dagger, a chair, a furred dressing-gown, a coil of rope and a cloak. Their bodies were unmarked by the explosion. Evidently the two men had noticed armed men surrounding the house, so climbed out of a window in an attempt to escape, but they had been discovered and smothered to death, perhaps with the dressing-gown or cloak, just before the house was put to gunpowder. Despite conflicting testimonies and an attempted cover-up, most historians today conclude that the men responsible were members of the Douglas clan or faction. Morton himself was not in Edinburgh that night, but he would have planned the murder, while his kinsmen – including Archibald Douglas – carried it out. Others were also involved: Bothwell was at the heart of the murder conspiracy; Huntly, Argyll and Maitland were strongly implicated. Moray might have known what was going on, but turned a blind eye. As for Mary, her reactions to the explosion and murder suggest her complete ignorance. Her astonishment and fear seem genuine; she acted as though she honestly believed that she, as well as Henry, was the intended victim of the gunpowder plot.

Rumour soon picked out Bothwell as the murderer, although fingers were also pointed at Moray and Morton. Mary began to be suspected as well because of her extraordinary conduct after the murder. Here she made many mistakes. Instead of acting conventionally, she waited five days before ordering her widow's weeds and the black taffeta to cover the walls and windows of her

The Aftermath of Darnley's Murder

RIGHT

Letter from Mary to Darnley's father, the Earl of Lennox, who had recently implored Mary to bring his son's murderers to justice. In this reply Mary thanks him for his good counsel and declares her intention to call a parliament. The letter is written by a clerk, but signed off by Mary as 'your good daughter Marie R'.
(British Library, Cotton Caligula B X, f. 408)

BELOW

Portrait of Matthew Stewart, 4th Earl of Lennox. Lennox had married Margaret Douglas, the niece of Henry VIII, in 1544. Their son, Henry, was born the following year. After Henry's murder, Lennox sought revenge and tried to bring the Earl of Bothwell to trial. In 1570 Lennox was chosen regent for his grandson, but was killed the next year.
(© Crown Copyright, 2006, Historic Scotland Images)

OPPOSITE

'Ane Declaratioun of the Lordis iust quarrel', 1567 by an unknown author. This verse is an example of the propaganda against Mary. The narrator here is listening to a conversation between two learned men, Philandrius and Eridielus. The latter asks 'what cause has the Lords of Scotland to take on an enterprise of such folie against the queen and her husband?' Philandrius then tells the story of Darnley's murder and Mary's immorality.
(British Library, Cotton Caligula C I, f. 14v)

Ohlandius to answer than him sped,
And this he said Eridielus vntill:
Gif that a freind with fairis away war led
Be wickit craft syne to sit war till ill,
Thocht the couet in that stait to byde still,
Zit in that caice his freindis of dewrie
Sould wis his weill and seik his libertie.

¶ And gif his fantasie war sa far infectie,
That to the treuth he could not bent his eir:
He sould not be in foly zit neglectit
Bot fairnes than sould mixit be with feir,
And gif all this could him na wysedome leir
Than acht he be of all puissance denude,
To do na euill gif he could do na gude.

¶ Than sen that bowdin bludy beist Bothwell,
Hes trayterously in myrk put downe our King:
His wyfe the Quene syne rauysset to him sell,
In fylthie lust throw cullour of wedding.
Thocht sho be witcheit wald in ruttery ring,
The Nobillis sould nether of thir enduire,
That lowne to leif, nor hir to be his huire.

¶ And gif the poysone in hir hart be sonkin,
That sho will not consent he puneist be:
Gif with his fylthie lust sho be sa dronkin,
That sho forzet office and honestie
Than man hir Nobillis of necessitie,
Cut of hir force quhill tresoun be reuengeit,
And this confusioun in ane ordour changeit.

¶ In priuat personnis sayis Eridielus,
I vnderstand thy taill is trew in deid:
Bot in Princes it is maie perrillous,
And few examplis thairof can I reid.
And in sic caice the subiectis all had neid,
Haill to concur with ane authoritie
Sic concurrence in Scotland nane I se.

¶ Ohlandius sayis brother than considder,
How fyrst began all dominatiounis:
Quhen euid pepill assemblit thame togidder
And maid thair Kingis be creatiounis.
In votis than war variatiounis,
I trow rycht few was chosin be the haill,
Bot he was King quhais pairtie did preuaill.

¶ Rycht sa gif Princes sa thame self abuse,
That of force subiectis man put to thair hand:
Guid men sould not than to reforme refuse,
Thocht all at anis concur not on thair band.
Namly gif Iustice on thair pairtie stand,
And in it I consent gif quha wald rackin rycht,
Sen God hes gein to thame baith strēch and mycht.

Zea thocht it war ane King for to depose,
For certaine crymis I think the subiectis may,
Or fylthy faultouris fast in prisone close,
Rather than lat ane haill countrie decay.
Thay sould not sture thocht sum men wald say nay
To ane purpose the haill will neuer conclude,
Thay haue aneuch, hes force and quarrell gude.

¶ May thay not put ane ordoure to the heid:
Quha in beginning did the heid vp mak
May thay not set ane better in the steid,
Gif it fra vice can not be callit bak.
Les this be done Realmes will ga to wrak,
Namely quhen that the cryme is sa patent
That nouther misters Iuge nor argument.

¶ As gif ane King his pepill wald betray,
And him and thame baith bring to seruitude:
He sould in this reformit be I say,
Naimly be Nobillis and be men of gude.
The Baliols cause considdir how it stude,
Quhat rycht had Robert Bruice him to expell:
Because to Ingland he subiect him sell.

¶ And now gif I durst speik without respect,
To huirmaisters, to murderers of Kingis:
To throtcutters our Realme was maid subiect,
Quha in thair malice proudely zit malingis.
Lat Nobill hartis considder all thir thingis,
Thay sall weill find that this puire natioun,
Greit mister had of reformatioun.

¶ Sic fylthie luste in Sardanapalus,
Sic crueltie in Nero did not ring:
Sic brutishe lyfe in Heliogabalus
Sic traytour mynde to slay his Lord and King,
In feirceir Phocas beist did neuer spring:
Sic beistly bowgrie Sodome hes not sene
As rang in him quha rewlit Realme and Quene.

¶ And sould the Nobill Barronis of this land
In boilis lurk and this mischeif behauld,
Quhair is the wittis wont to reule Scotlande
Go reid the buik, repeit the storyis auld,
King Euenus was keipit in strang hauld
And deit thair Conacus was inclosit,
First being dewlie for his fault deposit.

¶ For wickit lyfe imprisont was Ferquhaird,
Quha slew him self of proude melancolie,
Donald the fyst he gat the same renaird:
And Ethus did in prisone priuate die,
And gif ze list to go fra this countrie,
In euerie land examplis dois abound
Gif thay be socht thay may be eithlie found.

¶ For sic misordour proude Tarquinius
Was the last King that euer did ring in Rome,
For lyke crymes the tyran Claudius:
Lost his stait and gat deid for his dome,
To speik of Nero now I haue na tome
Off Commodus, Caius and Caracall,
It war to lang for to discriue the fall.

¶ Quhat sorow into Naples than was sene,
Quha knawis the story cleirly thair may reid,
Quhen Charlis dochter Ieane that came Quene
Baith honestie forzet and womanheid,
Hir husband and hir cousing put to deid,
Syne with his Barrio band ane new mariage,
Allace this sample seruis ouer weill our age.

apartments. She allowed Henry to be buried quietly at night instead of giving him the state funeral that a King of Scotland deserved. She failed to observe the forty days' strict seclusion expected of a widow, and instead attended a wedding feast on the morning of 11 February. She also went twice to Seton, ten miles east of Edinburgh, for short stays. The first time, on 16 February, her ostensible purpose was to soothe her nerves, which admittedly were shot to pieces. On the second occasion, in late February, she was accompanied by Bothwell, and it was reported that they played at archery together. Although Mary's unseemly behaviour was by no means evidence of her guilt, it badly harmed her reputation, and she showed poor judgement in taking no account of public opinion. Even though she did not grieve for her dead husband, it was important that she should perform the traditional formalities of mourning to the letter.

To make matters worse, Mary did little to bring the murderers to justice. A handsome reward of £2,000 and other inducements were offered for information about the crime, but no proper investigation took place. This was hardly surprising given that so many of Mary's lords were involved in the murder and that Bothwell, as sheriff of Edinburgh, was responsible for mounting the inquiry. Nonetheless, her failure to discover and arrest the principal conspirators attracted unfavourable comment in Scotland and abroad: both Elizabeth I and Catherine de' Medici exhorted her to prosecute Henry's murderers energetically and thereby save her

honour. Mary, however, ignored their advice and instead showed favour to the leading suspects. Morton was allowed to return to court. As for Bothwell, not only did she help him build up a strong military presence in Edinburgh and add to his offices, but she also gave him small but significant tokens of her esteem, not least the finest horses and clothes of her late husband.

The most plausible explanation for this inappropriate conduct is that Mary was unaware of Bothwell's role in the murder, and that she continued to hold Moray responsible. She did seem to retain the belief that her half-brother had intended her to die at Kirk o' Field alongside Henry and then seize her throne. But it is also possible that Mary discovered Bothwell's role soon after the murder and decided he had acted out of devotion to her person and in the interests of the Crown.

OPPOSITE
Anonymous ballad lamenting the death of Darnley and calling for revenge, 1567. In this printed verse, 'Heir followis the testament and tragedie of umqwhile [sometime] King Henrie Stewart of gude memorie', the words are supposedly spoken by the dead king. In verse twelve Mary is implicitly compared to the legendary Greek queen Clytemnestra, who murdered her husband Agamemnon to marry her lover, Egistus. (British Library, Cotton Caligula C I, f. 26)

Heir followis the testament and tragedie of

unquhile King Henrie Stewart of gude memorie

Henry Stewart, unquhile of Scotland King,
Sumtyme in houpe, with reverence to King:
Within this Realme in dew obedience,
Casting with ane attoure all eirdlie thing
...a was the rutte quhairof I did spring,
...honour to liue be kyndelie allyance:
...rand in hir sic faith and confidence,
...gland I left, seducit be Ignorance,
...otland I socht, in houpe for to get hir:
...hilk I may rew, as now is cum the chance,
...d vthers learne by me experience
...tyme be war, fra ainis the work misset hir.

Sumtyme scho thocht, I was sa amiabill,
...perfyte, plesand, and sa dilectabill:
...nit with luif, scho luid me by all wycht,
...m tyme to schaw effectioun fanorabill,
...ratise it me with giftis honorabill,
...nid me ze knaw, baith Lord, Duik, Erle & Knycht:
...m tyme in mynde scho praisit me sa hycht,
...sand all vther, hir bedfellow brycht
...esit me to be, and maid me zour King:
...an was I thocht happy into menis sycht
...d puir anis did pryse thair maker of mycht
...at send thame ane Stewart sa kyndelie to King.

Thus quhen scho had avancit me in estate,
...for to pleis I set my haill consait:
...hilk now is cause of my rakles ruyne,
...Acheeious luife quhilk kindlit ouer hait,
...uld hes it cuild, and sylit me with dissait
...angeit my corps into this present pyne,
...t onelie zow Lordis causand me to tyne,
...t als allace fra my trew God declyne,
...thome I imbracit, for plesoure of hir Eyes
...ellie thairfoir, I haue deservit this syne,
...ha for hir saik denyit the God devine
...at did me bring fra plesoure to distres.

Backwart fra God my Spirite fra scho wylit,
...plie with darknes my spreit scho ouersylit,
...Princelie pretence began to decay,
...ine houpe in hir my restoun exilit,
...truethles toung my honoure defylit
...doing in deid scho gart me deny,
...a credite I crakit, kyndnes brak tay,
...man wald trow the worde I did say,
...leigis me left, persauand hir Ire
...gland I left, and help was away
...maid hir scurge to plaigue me for ay,
...war the scurge he cast not in the fyre.

Thus was I than to doloure destinat,
...serabill man and Prince infortunat,
...homlie in sorow and plungeit in cair:
...m tyme in mynde with anger agitat,
...m tyme in Spirit pansive and fatigat,
...sand the meine mycht meis hir euer mair,
...m tyme with doloure drewin in dispair,
...ciand the warld, welth and weilfair,
...d I desirit hir fallset to fle,
...m tyme in mynd thinkand the contrare,
...m vincouthe baiage I purpoisit prepare,
...t not sa vncouth as was prepairit for me.

Into the tyme of this my extasie,
...hen I was in this fearfull fantasie,
...ch [Reverie] fair, and wylie wordis discreie,
...ho come to me with greit humilitie:
...mentand fair my greit calamitie,
...langsum lyfe, and fair for nentit Spirite,

Bromefand with ane faithfull hart contreit,
In tyme to cum, with reuerence me treit
To my degre, in honoure, luife and peace,
Traistand into hir meekie wordis sweit,
My hairt and lyfe into hir handis compleit,
I put, and past vnto the Sacrifice.

Quhat sall I wryte, how I was troublit thair,
I wat it wald mak ony haill hairt fair,
For to renolue my tristfull tragidie,
How that thay boucheouris blew me in the air,
And stranglit me, I shame for to declair:
Nouther to God, nor honoure hauand Ee,
I houpit weill to haue na ennymie,
Into this Realme fra my narinitie,
Thair was na man, quhome to I did offend,
Dissauit far I sand the contrarie,
Off Tygeris quholpis fosterit in tyrannie,
Ane treuthles troup hes drewin me to this end.

O faithles flock, denuide of godlynes,
O Serpentis seid, nurisheit in wickitnes,
Fosteraris of falset, huirdome and harlatrie,
Mantenaris of murther, witchecraft expres,
Tresoun amang zow dois daylic incres:
Lawrie is banist, Justice and equitie,
Quhat sall I wryte of zoure wyle vanitie?
On falset is foundit zour haill felicitie,
Zour Castellis nor townis, sall not zow defend,
God hes persauit zour infidelitie,
And schortlie will plaigue zour crewell tyrannie,
Off zoure schort solace sorow salbe the end.

Quhat hairt so hard for perie will not bleid?
Vnhat breist can beir bot man lament my deid?
Quhat toung sa thrall in silence suir can rest?
To se ane saule in sorow sowsit but feid,
Ane saikles Lambe, ane innocent but dreid,
Taine be consent of thame be luiffit best:
Furth of his bed with doloure to be drest,
By thrawart malice and murther manifest,
Jugeit by Law, and hangit syne but doine,
Sair it was to se zoure Prince with murther prest:
Sairast I say him in his place possest,
The deid that did, than Burrio, now Brydegrome.

O wickit [person] vennomus of nature,
Serpentis of kynde, thocht cumlie seme zour stature
As heir my end reheirsit dois record,
Vnstabill ioy, full of aduersitie,
In mynde malicious attoure all creature,
Quhais malice taine, for euer dois indure:
Teichit be experience, sa may I testifie,
Zoure craftie consaitis cleirlit with flatterie,
And mylde meiknes sylit with subtilitie,
At Medeais helteris to bring vs in zour net,
Gude deidis of auld gois furth of memorie,
The ruite of euill remaines but remedie,
Ay in zoure mynde sum vengance quhill ze get.

For Dawyis deid in [...] sa prentit
Consauit haitrent, daylie mair augmentit,
Meik war his wordis, thocht greit was his greenance
Oft at command, to mak hir weill contentit,
In pouertie and paine my self fra court absentit
Paine could not pleis hir, nor zit obedience,
Persaue of [...] the malice and mischance,
Quhair [...] anis gettis in hir gouernance,
Sic sylit subiectis felterit in hir snair:
Wisdome is exilit, and prudent purueyance,
Noblines and honour, defacit be ignorance,
And vertew banist, fra shame pas shed of hair.

This sentence trew we may persaue in deid,
In sindrie authouris quha lykis for to reid,
In luiffis raige, as storyis doig reheirs,
The crewell work of wretcheit womanheid,
We may persaue in Scylla so succeid:
For Minos luife, hir Father gaif na grace,
Deianira hir husband Hercules,
For Nessus saik, maist crewellie allace
Brocht to mischeif, for all his vassalage,
And Clytemnestra for Egistus face.
Agamemnon the mychtie King of Greice,
Hir husband slew, so vyle was hir vsage.

Off Ancus Martius we reid the greit mischance,
Quha rang in Rome in proude preheminance,
Slaine be Lucinio at Tanaquillis procuise,
Samson also for manheid and prudence,
All Israell that had in gouernance:
Dalila defauit in vnder couertoure:
Quhairfoir lat men be war and keip thame suire,
Fra wemenis vennome, vnder faithles figure,
And gif na wyfe thair counsall for to keip,
For as the woirme that workis vnder cuire
At leuth the tre consumis that is duire,
So wemen men, fra thay in credite creip.

I speik not but pruise, quhilk I may sairlie rew,
Quhat lyfe did thoill, my deid dois try it trew,
My fragill fortowne, sa faithles hes bene heir,
Wald God the day that I thee Scotland knew,
Atropus the tireid had cut, lachesis drew,
So sould not felt the change of fortownes cheir,
My kingdome cair, my wealth was ay in weir,
My state vnstabill, me drew fra Godis feir,
My plesoure pirkis my paine ay to prouoke,
My solace sorow sobbing to asteir,
My ryches, powertie, power to empire,
My [...] hes now put out the smoke.

Quhat warldlie ioy in earth may lang induice,
Or quhat estate may heir him self assuire?
For to conse tue his lyfe in sicernes,
Quha may sustene the perrillous auentuire?
Off fals fortowne inconstant and vnsuire:
Or quhair sall men find steidfast stabilnes?
All warldlie blis is mixt with bitternes,
Springand with ioy, endand with wretchitnes,
Quhairfoir let Princes pryde thame not expres
In warldlie welth in pomp nor worthynes,
Bot stablishe thair strenth, with Dauid on the Lord.

In earth thairfoir sen nocht is parmanent,
My soule to God I left omnipotent,
My Bab and Childe vnder the counsallis cuire,
To zow my Lordis of my deid Innocent,
For to reuenge I left in Testament,
My saikles bluid, my murther and iniure,
Thocht Princes wald be falset zow alluire,
Hurt not zour honouris, the samin to smuire,
First luik to God, syne to zour libertie,
Think weill suppois my death ze wald induire,
Gif Rubbers King na subiect salbe suire,
Mair nor the Sheip in Foxis companie.

FINIS.

Imprentit at
Edinburgh be Robert Lekprenik.
Anno Do. 1567.

Whatever her reasons, Mary was politically unwise in failing to distance herself from Bothwell, the man seen by everyone else as the prime suspect in the wicked crime, and she consequently allowed herself to become the target of malicious and damaging accusations. In Edinburgh, gossips soon coupled her name with Bothwell's, and placards were pinned up that libelled them both. One showed a sword next to Mary's initials and a mallet besides Bothwell's, signifying that they were both the assassins of the dead king. Another, perhaps the most notorious, was an explicitly sexual picture of a mermaid and a hare. The mermaid, labelled MR, had a crown on her head and held a rolled-up net in her left hand and a large sea anemone (signifying female genitalia) in her right. Below the mermaid, and ready to be caught in her net, was a hare (the heraldic emblem of the Hepburns) placed within a circle of seventeen swords (phallic symbols). For those who did not pick up the allusion, the letters JH were placed inside the circle to identify Bothwell by his name, James Hepburn.

Lennox may have been behind some of the libels. He was certainly furious at the failure to bring his son's murderers to justice, and accused Bothwell and other lesser men of the deed. In response to his accusations, a private trial was scheduled for 12 April 1567. For his own security Lennox took three thousand men with him to attend it, for he had heard that Edinburgh was filled with thousands of Bothwell's armed supporters. When he reached Linlithgow, however, he was informed

The names of such of the Nobilitie as subscribe
the Band so far as John Read might remem
of whome I had this copie beemo his owne
hand beemo comonly termed in Scotland
Aynsleis supper

The Erles of   Lords
Murray   Boyd
Argile   Seyton
Huntley   Sinclar
Cassells   Semple
Morton   oliphant
Sutherland   ogleuy
Rothos   Rosse hacat
Glencarn   Carlele
Cathnesse   Herris
                      Hume
                      Eumermeth
                      Eglinton subscribe not but slipp away

that the law would permit him to take only six followers into the town. Not daring to proceed, he asked for a postponement of the trial, but his request was ignored. The trial was a travesty of justice: Lennox did not appear to give evidence, and after seven hours discussing legal technicalities, the jury acquitted the accused. Mary was rightly blamed for letting the trial go ahead in circumstances that made it impossible for Lennox's case to be heard. Less fairly, though, many observers also believed that she was protecting Bothwell from justice, whereas in reality she had lost control of her government.

At the parliament that met on 14 April 1567 Mary again behaved unwisely by giving prominence to Bothwell. He carried the sceptre in the procession to the Tolbooth, and the sword of honour back to Holyrood. One piece of business parliament enacted was the ratification of the grant of Dunbar Castle to Bothwell on account of his 'great and manifold good service'.[58] At the same time, the ancestral lands and titles of Morton, Huntly, Argyll,

Moray and others were confirmed. It looked suspiciously as if Mary was paying off those who had participated in a plot to murder her estranged husband. At the end of the session she ratified the Acts of the 1560 Reformation Parliament, which, until then, she had consistently refused to do. Her surrender on this point also looked suspicious. Many later assumed that she was offering this concession to the Protestant lords in order to buy their support for her marriage to Bothwell. Given that there is no evidence that she intended marriage to the earl at this point, it is far more likely that she was simply trying to win over Protestant public opinion in Edinburgh.

By this time Bothwell had set his sights on Mary. He and his wife had already agreed to an amicable divorce, and since they were both Protestants, it could easily be obtained on the grounds of his adultery with a long-time mistress. Mary's consent to the match, Bothwell believed, would be easily secured as she was so dependent upon him for advice and support. All he needed, therefore, was the agreement of the leading lords and churchmen. On the evening of 19 April he received it. He put before them a document, known as 'Ainslie's Tavern bond', which accepted his innocence in Henry's murder and recommended Mary to take him as a husband. Eight earls, eleven barons, six bishops and the Archbishop of St Andrews signed the bond, but there were significant omissions. Moray's name did not appear on the document, as he had gone abroad in March, while Argyll, Maitland, Atholl and Sir James Melville seem

to have refused their signatures. Morton did sign, but only on terms that severely limited Bothwell's powers and denied him the title of king.

On 20 April Bothwell joined Mary at Seton, showed her the bond and proposed marriage. To his amazement, she turned him down. Undeterred, Bothwell decided to take immediate and bold action to secure her consent before opposition to the match from the nobility could grow. On Monday 21 April Mary travelled to Stirling to see her son. Two days later she went to Linlithgow, and the following morning (Thursday 24 April) she set out for Edinburgh accompanied by some thirty men, including Huntly, Maitland and Sir James Melville. On the way they were stopped by Bothwell and a band of about eight hundred armed men, who wanted to divert them to his castle at Dunbar. Some of Mary's servants were prepared to defend her with arms from this abduction, for no one in her entourage believed Bothwell's excuse that it was too dangerous for them to return to Edinburgh. Mary, however, would offer no resistance, saying that she wanted to avoid bloodshed. She then travelled the forty or so miles to Dunbar without trying to escape. She remained there for twelve days, until 6 May, when Bothwell took her back to Edinburgh as his intended bride.

Debates occurred at the time and afterwards about what really happened. Was Mary kidnapped by Bothwell, or was she complicit in the abduction, as one of her captors claimed? The Spanish ambassador in England reported suspicions at Elizabeth's court that 'the whole thing has been arranged so that, if anything comes of the marriage, the Queen may make out that she was forced into it'.[59] Were these suspicions accurate? If not, what then happened at Dunbar? Was she persuaded by argument to marry Bothwell? Was she perhaps seduced by him, or did he rape her there, as Melville claimed? Historians disagree on all these points.

In my view it is unlikely that Mary colluded in the abduction. If she had wanted to marry Bothwell, she could just as easily have accepted his proposal at Seton and answered any criticisms by presenting Ainslie's Tavern bond and pointing out that her lords had requested the match. It is true that her lack of resistance contrasts with the courage and resourcefulness she had demonstrated earlier in her reign, and suggests a staged event, but her timidity was understandable given that her small retinue was greatly outnumbered by Bothwell's force. Besides, the intense emotional strain experienced since the murder of Rizzio had affected her badly, leaving her lacking in energy, frequently ill, and unable to think clearly. In these circumstances, her submissiveness can be readily understood. Whether or not she was raped is more difficult to answer. Some historians think it unlikely, but Melville was very clear on this point, and Bothwell was certainly capable of such a brutal action. He could well have decided on possessing her body to force her into marriage; and Mary's agreement to marry him at Dunbar

also makes psychological sense if she had been subjected to the force and dishonour of non-consensual sex. As Melville commented, 'The Queen could not but marry him, seeing he had ravished her and lain with her against her will.'[60]

With Mary's agreement to matrimony secured, Bothwell expedited the arrangements to annul his existing fifteen-month-old marriage. His divorce obtained, the banns were read under duress by Knox's assistant at St Giles on 9 May 1567. Three days later, Mary created Bothwell Duke of Orkney and Lord of Shetland, and on the morning of 15 May the couple were married by a Protestant minister in the Great Hall at Holyrood. Unsurprisingly, the wedding was a quiet affair: it was sparsely attended and there were no masques or entertainments, just a wedding dinner. Mary wore a black taffeta gown trimmed with braid for the ceremony, and afterwards changed into a yellow gown. It was not until 23 May that a pageant was put on to celebrate the marriage.

OVERLEAF

Diagram of the military engagement at Carberry Hill, June 1567. Mary is shown twice: on the right, where she is riding side-saddle amidst the army of 'the quine's campe' with the royal banner of lion rampant, and also in the centre, where she is on her way to parley with the confederate lords.

Also labelled are William Kirkcaldy of Grange ('lard of Grang', centre, above Mary), Lord Hume (centre, below Mary) and the Earl of Morton (left). The rebel lords display two banners, both showing the corpse of Darnley, and one bearing the words 'Judg and reveng my cas o Lord'. (National Archives, Kew)

Saltpeston

the quinck campe

Saltpeston

olmston

Mary's third marriage brought her no more happiness than her second. In public she and Bothwell showed each other appropriate respect, but in private they rowed incessantly. Bothwell was as possessive a husband as Darnley had been, and flew into violent rages whenever Mary showed liking for a male or female courtier. Melville reported that not one day passed in their married life when she had not 'shed abundance of salt tears'.[61] Personal differences apart, the marriage was given little opportunity to succeed; from its outset the couple were under great pressure owing to hostile public opinion and an ominous political situation.

Even before the wedding, Bothwell's allies were falling away, partly because of old enmities, partly from new jealousies at his promotion. On 1 May 1567 Morton, Argyll, Atholl and Mar signed a new bond, calling themselves the 'Confederate Lords' and declaring their aims were to free the queen from Bothwell's influence, preserve Prince James, and pursue those who had murdered Darnley. This bond was followed up by a second one after the marriage. The lords made Stirling their base and were joined there by new nobles and gentlemen. On 6 June Maitland, who had quarrelled with Bothwell at Dunbar, defected to the lords with his wife, Mary Fleming. The new captain of Edinburgh Castle, Sir James Balfour, initially stayed in his place, but treacherously, he too went over to the rebels' side. By this time the confederates numbered thirty and had raised an army of some three thousand men.

On 6 June 1567 Bothwell and Mary left Holyrood for the safety of Borthwick Castle, which lay about twelve miles south-east of Edinburgh. Four days later a group of rebels surrounded the castle. Knowing it could not withstand a siege, Bothwell slipped away to gather reinforcements. Mary, though, had to endure insults hurled at her when she refused to abandon her husband and return to Edinburgh with them. The following night, disguised 'in man's apparel',[62] she made her own escape, and, after meeting up with Bothwell, she rode with him to Dunbar. Her blood up, Mary was determined to confront the rebels who had occupied Edinburgh. On Saturday 14 June she led her army towards Leith. Dressed in borrowed clothes – 'a red petticoat, sleeves tied with points', a velvet hat and a muffler – she looked a strange sight. 'The queen's apparel in the field was after the attire and fashion of the women of Edinburgh' was the report that reached London.[63] Yet, despite her less than regal appearance, some five hundred or so men joined Mary and her small force of 260 soldiers as they rode towards Edinburgh. At Haddington she met Bothwell, who commanded two thousand more. Together they went to Seton, where they stayed the night.

The next morning Morton and Atholl led out the rebel army of four thousand men towards Musselburgh. The banner held at the front of their procession depicted the corpse of Darnley lying under a tree with his son kneeling beneath him and the words: 'Judge and avenge my cause, O Lord'. A few hours later, Mary and Bothwell led out the royal army to take up a commanding position on Carberry Hill, two miles south-east of Musselburgh. It was a very hot day and neither side was keen on a fight. An attempt was therefore made at mediation, in which Mary was asked to desert Bothwell, the murderer of her second husband. Mary refused, pointing out that she had married the earl with the lords' approval, as shown by the bond they had signed. Next, both sides agreed to settle the matter by single combat, and Bothwell stepped forward to fight to the death against Morton or Lord Lindsay as his proxy. Mary then intervened and forbade the duel for reasons that are unclear and difficult to explain. One possibility, though, is that she suspected she was pregnant and did not want the father of her second child to be killed, as the father of her first had been.

By this time a battle was no longer feasible as most of Mary's army had drifted away during the hot day of inactivity, and she was left with only some four hundred men. So Mary had to choose between flight and negotiation with the rebel lords. Although Bothwell urged their retreat to Dunbar where they could raise more troops, Mary chose to make terms, accepting the lords' offer of a safe conduct for Bothwell in return for her surrender and a promise that they would treat her honourably. Her capitulation is difficult to comprehend, but most probably she was worn down at the end of a long, exhausting and emotional day, and wanted to avoid full-scale civil war. She thought too that she could trust the good faith of the rebel lords. Their chief negotiator, Sir

William Kirkcaldy, the Laird of Grange, had assured her that they were not attacking her crown, but simply wanted justice done for the murder of her second husband. If so, Mary had nothing to fear; and if they did break their word and attempt to depose her, Bothwell would still be free to take up arms again.

Mary was escorted back to Edinburgh in a terrible state: weeping, dirty, dishevelled, and her ears ringing with insults hurled at her, first by the rebel soldiers and then the crowds at the side of the road. 'Burn the whore' was a common refrain. Humiliated and furious at her treatment, 'she hath given to diverse very bitter words',[64] reserving the strongest for Lindsay, whom she threatened to hang. Although understandable, such threats were unwise; to keep her throne she needed to seem calm and accommodating, not angry and unforgiving.

In Edinburgh, Mary was kept under custody at the Provost's house for a night. The next morning she went to the window, crying out that she was being kept a prisoner, and she appeared so distraught that she moved the crowd below to 'pity and compassion'.[65] That evening she was hurried off towards the small and bleak castle of Lochleven on a tiny island in the middle of a loch near Kinross, thirty miles north of Edinburgh. Her accommodation was primitive and her custodians indifferent to her plight. The main warder was Sir William Douglas, half-brother to Moray and the cousin of Morton, but Lindsay, who had assisted in the murder of Rizzio, was also present.

Portrait of King James VI of Scotland, c.1574, attributed to Rowland Lockey after Arnold von Bronckhorst. James, aged about eight years old here, is shown with a sparrowhawk perched on his outstretched hand. (National Portrait Gallery, London)

First page of a proclamation against the supporters of Mary, dated May 1568. Written in the name of King James VI, it calls Mary's supporters 'treasonable conspirators and troublers of the realm', and refers to James as the 'lawful king'. The troubles of the realm are blamed on Mary and Bothwell: 'Our father lately murdered and the Queen our Mother coupled with him that was the chief author of that mischievous deed'. (British Library, Cotton Caligula C 1, f. 78)

Ane proclamatioun anent the

tressonable Conspiratouris and trublaris of the tranquillitie of the commoun welth now laitlie assemblit aganis the kingis grace authoritie.

Iames be the grace of God king of Scottis. To our louittis Martine Uddart ormond Purseuät, Hectour Trohope Maser, Williame Lawsone Messingeris, our Schireffis in that part coniunctlie and seueral-lie, specialie constitute, greting, Forsamekle, as it is weill and noto-riouslie knawin vnto all our louing and faithfull subiectis, how that efter the greit trublis raisit in our tender age, throw the occasioun of the lait abhominabill murther committit in the persoun of vmquhile our derrest Father. It plesit the gudnes of God throw his mercy to grant vnto our sai-dis liegis efter the punissing and banischement of certane the cheif conspiratouris and executuris of the foirsaid murther, ane repose and quyetnes, and ane happy stait of go-uernment in this our Realme be renunciatioun and dimissioun of the Crowne in oue handis be our derrest mother, appreuit, confirmit, and ratifyit be the thre Estatis of our Realme, lauchfullie conuenit in Parliament, and be the godlie and verteous ministrati-oun of Iustice begun and practysit be sic as war lauchfully callit and appointit vnto the Regiment of vs, our Realme and liegis, to the greit consort and quyetnes of all sic as tenderit the honour and glorie of God, ye quyetnes and repose of all our faithfull subiect the mantenance of godly and vpryçht leuaris, and the punischement of all criminallis & notorious transgressouris. Quhill now of lait that certane tressonable, seditious, and wickit personis mouit outher be particular haitrent aganis vtheris our gude and faith-full subiectis, or than allurit be esperance of sum particular gayne, proffeit, or auancemēt, quhilk thay pretend to obtene be menis of the trubling of our obedience and authoritie, a inquyeting of the repose and quyet state of our gude and faithfull subiectis, hes mouit & perswadit diuers and sindrie our liegis to conuene thame selfis togidder tressonabilly a-ganis vs and our authoritie, and for impesching and estaying of vs, and our derrest cou-sing James Erle of Murray Lord Abirnethie, Regent of our Realme and liegis, in the trew and faithfull administratioun of Iustice, & punischeing of transgressouris, quhairin we had sa happylie begun, to the greit greif of, vs our said Regent, and all our faithfull subiectis, quha sa lang bad lukit for the same without tymous remeid be fundin thairfoir. And becauſe the saidis conspyratouris as hes appeirit to vs and our said derrest cousing, intendis sa far as in thame lyis to vsurpe and oppone thame selfis aganis our persoun, power, and authoritie be way of deid and armis vnder the pretence and cullour of our said derrest mother, quha hes not only denudit hir handis thairof in our fauouris, & we establischit thairin, as is weil knawin to our Estatis quha hes approuin the said dimissi-oun. Bot als our saidis thre Estatz in respect thairof, and for diuers vtheris greit & maist wechtie causis knawin and perfitely prouin vnto thame be thair sessiament in Parliamēt, hes fundin and declarit the same lauchfull and perfite in all respectis. Now we ar cōstra-nit to mantene and fortifie be force of armes our persoun and royall authoritie, aganis sic tressonabill conspyratouris and vnnaturall subiectis to vs thair natiue Prince and King.

For the first fortnight of her captivity Mary slumped into desperation, barely able to take any nourishment, but then, during early July, she slowly began to take exercise and recover. Sometime in the middle of the month, however, she miscarried, and soon afterwards, on 24 July 1567, while (according to her own later account) she was in a state of great weakness, Lindsay forced her to sign a note of abdication in favour of her son and to nominate Moray as regent. Mary had first resisted, but submitted when Lindsay threatened to slit her throat or throw her into the loch, but she made clear her belief that an agreement made under duress had no legal status. Shortly afterwards she fell ill again.

Meanwhile, in Edinburgh, the rebel lords had seized her valuable property – personal as well as state – and mounted a propaganda campaign against her. They justified her imprisonment by falsely accusing her of breaking the agreement with them and writing to Bothwell. They also criticized her for not consenting to a divorce, and claimed she intended to escape to him and raise troops again. In truth, Morton and his allies at Carberry had had no intention of letting her go free, for their security and position depended on her incarceration and deposition. Mary was approaching the age of twenty-five, when, according to Scottish custom, she could recall land and titles given out during her minority, and they feared she would take this opportunity to wreak vengeance on them. Furthermore, for obvious reasons, as Darnley's murderers, they needed full control over the

investigation into the Kirk o' Field explosion that they planned would pin the murder on both Bothwell and Mary.

Bothwell was declared an outlaw and rebel on 17 July 1567. With his lands sequestered and his adherents drifting away, the earl abandoned his attempt to raise an army against the rebel lords. Pursued by Kirkcaldy of Grange, he fled to the Orkneys, then to the Shetland Islands, from where he escaped to Norway in late August 1567. Arrested there, he was sent to the Castle of Copenhagen as prisoner of the King of Denmark, and moved in 1575 to Dragsholm Castle, some sixty miles to the west, where he died in 1578. Meanwhile, in Scotland during his months of flight, Bothwell's servants were hunted down and, under threat of torture, they confessed their part in the murder of Darnley. One of them, Bothwell's tailor George Dalgliesh, was later said to have handed over a silver casket (decorated with a crown) from under his bed, in which were found letters incriminating Mary in adultery with Bothwell and the death of her husband.

With his mother out of the way, the thirteen-month-old James VI was crowned on 29 July 1567 in the parish church of Stirling. The ceremony was Protestant, and Knox preached the sermon. On 11 August the Earl of Moray returned to Scotland, and a few days afterwards he visited Mary at Lochleven. In two emotional interviews she reproached her half-brother for her ill treatment, and he berated her for her foolish behaviour, which had left her reputation in tatters. Terrified by his judgemental attitude, Mary agreed to Moray being regent, and he left her to her fate.

After Moray's installation on 22 August, the conditions of Mary's imprisonment improved somewhat. Now joined by Mary Seton and a small domestic staff, she was able to embroider, play cards, write letters, even dance to the fiddle and bagpipes, as well as to think about escape. In the spring of 1568 she smuggled out letters to Catherine de' Medici, begging for troops to be sent to free her: 'it is by force alone that I can be delivered from here'.[66] Around the same time, Mary made an unsuccessful attempt at flight when she slipped out of the castle disguised as a laundress, but her identity was soon discovered by a boatman. On Sunday 2 May 1568, however, she did make a successful getaway thanks to the efforts of two insiders who fell under her spell: George Douglas, the younger brother of the custodian, who had hopes of becoming her fourth husband, and an orphaned kinsman, the sixteen-year-old Willie Douglas. Willie let Mary, disguised as a countrywoman, out of the castle and put her into a boat, which took her to the shore where George was waiting with horses. Mary Seton stayed behind, pretending to be the captive queen.

Over the next week men flocked to the queen. Soon Mary had an army of about six thousand men led by numerous lords, including Huntly, Seton, Argyll and the Hamiltons. Some of these lords (such as Argyll) rallied to her because they had always been uneasy about her deposition; others (such as the Hamiltons) were incensed by the elevation of Moray to the regency. Faced with defections from his camp, Moray immediately ordered a muster and rode out to meet the enemy in battle. On Thursday 13 May Mary's army met Moray's at the small village of Langside, just outside Glasgow. Despite its superiority in numbers, her force was routed after only forty-five minutes. Mary, who was watching the catastrophic engagement from a nearby hill, fled southwards, determined not to be captured again. Guided by Lord Herries through the Lowlands, she rode her horses hard, covering sixty miles the first day, until she reached Dumfries. Continuing onwards, she slept in the open country, drank sour milk and ate oatmeal without bread. At last she reached the Castle of Terregles, owned by the loyal Lord Maxwell. There, against the advice of her supporters, she decided to go into England and seek aid from Elizabeth. During the afternoon of 16 May 1568, Mary, accompanied by sixteen companions, boarded a small fishing vessel and crossed the Solway Firth into England. She had high hopes that she would be received by her cousin at court, and expected too that aid would be forthcoming. Once again, she was deluded, and this error of judgement proved to be the most disastrous mistake of her life. By leaving her followers in Scotland leaderless, she severely weakened their chances of eventual victory against the rebels. Even worse, she placed herself in the hands of her enemies and was never to be free again.

CHAPTER FIVE

Early Years in England
1568–1572

A FTER A FOUR-HOUR journey across the Solway
Firth, Mary landed at the small Cumberland port
of Workington early on the evening of 16 May
1568. Conveyed to the nearby Workington Hall, she
immediately wrote a letter to Elizabeth describing her
plight and begging for assistance. Without clothes,
money or horses, Mary probably hoped to stay in the
comfortable hall until Elizabeth either granted her
licence to come to London or provided her with an army
to recover the Scottish throne. However, on the following
day the English queen's representative in the area arrived
with an armed guard to escort Mary on a thirty-mile
journey to the border fortress of Carlisle Castle.

On hearing the news of Mary's arrival, Elizabeth's first
instinct was to bring the fugitive queen to her court and
proffer her aid. The previous year she had been outraged
when learning of Mary's imprisonment and deposition;
in her view, the Scottish Confederate Lords had 'no
warrant nor authority by the law of God or man to be as
superiors, judges or vindicators over their prince and
sovereign'.[67] Such conduct, she believed, challenged the
very principle of monarchical government and set a
dangerous precedent. Consequently, she refused point-
blank to recognize James VI as king, and, indeed, was
only dissuaded from intervening on Mary's behalf in

OPPOSITE
*Portrait of Mary Queen of
Scots, c.*1610 after Nicholas
Hilliard. This portrait is
based on Hilliard's 1578
miniature of the queen,
and is one of a number of
similar versions produced
during the reign of her son,
James I. To emphasize her
Catholicism she is wearing
a crucifix around her neck,
and an elaborate gold Latin
cross and rosary attached
to her waist.
(National Portrait Gallery,
London)

1567 when Cecil and other councillors convinced her that English interference might well encourage the lords to kill their royal prisoner. Despite conciliar disapproval, Elizabeth did communicate her deep concern for Mary's safety to the Scottish lords, a message that may well have saved the deposed queen's life. Now, in 1568, Cecil and his fellow councillors again talked Elizabeth out of providing Mary with any assistance. Although they harked on Mary's sexual immorality and guilt in her husband's murder, their real concern was to protect the interests of Protestant England. These, they believed, would be greatly furthered if Moray and the Anglophile lords were left to govern Scotland and bring up the young James as a Protestant. But what was to be done with Mary? It was clear to Cecil and his colleagues that she could not be allowed to roam free in England, where she might build up a party of Catholic sympathizers, nor could she be permitted to travel abroad to France or Spain, from where she could incite a Catholic crusade. In their view, the best possible, though certainly not ideal, solution was to detain Mary in custody far away from Elizabeth's court. The difficulty was in selling this policy to Elizabeth.

Reluctantly accepting Cecil's advice that it would be unwise and inappropriate for her to meet the defamed fugitive, Elizabeth denied Mary a personal interview until such time as her innocence in the charges of adultery and murder was established and her reputation thereby restored. In the meantime, she sent

her councillor, Sir Francis Knollys (pronounced 'knowles'), to Carlisle Castle to act as one of Mary's temporary custodians. As a fervent anti-Catholic, Knollys was expected to show little sympathy towards his charge, but in fact he soon found himself succumbing to Mary's vitality, vulnerability and charm, although he did his best to maintain a hard line towards her. 'Surely she is a rare woman,' he wrote to Cecil: she was natural in her manners, had few airs, except for demanding acknowledgement of her royal estate, and showed 'a disposition to speak much, to be bold, to be pleasant and to be very familiar'. She also seemed attractively feminine and sensitive; when, for example, he spoke to her harshly, tears filled her eyes and he ended up comforting her.

Mary stayed in Carlisle for six weeks. There she was also in the custody of Lord Henry Scrope, Elizabeth's lord warden of the Western March, and attended by his wife Margaret, sister to the Duke of Norfolk. As time went by, companions and servants from Scotland drifted towards Carlisle, and for a while Mary's establishment touched a hundred. Mary Seton was one of those who joined Mary, and thanks to her hairdressing skills and use of wigs, the Scottish queen began to take on a more regal look. Her hair had needed special attention since it had been cropped as a form of disguise during her flight after the battle of Langside. In the summer Mary's belongings reached her from Lochleven, and she was then able to dress more fittingly for a queen and sit under an embroidered cloth of estate that denoted her royal status. Despite these growing conveniences, life at Carlisle was unquestionably dull. Mary filled her days sewing and writing letters to Elizabeth and other potential supporters, but was rarely able to take exercise owing to a lack of horses and her warders' fears that she might escape over the nearby Scottish border. Mary was effectively a prisoner. Her windows were heavily barred and guards accompanied her everywhere, while Knollys supervised her visitors and refused to allow English Catholics into her presence. Under this regime, her most noteworthy entertainment was watching a two-hour game of football played by twenty of her retinue.

It was not long before Elizabeth ordered Mary's transfer to Bolton Castle in north Yorkshire, where there was less danger of her escape. Bolton was Scrope's heavily fortified seat, set in an isolated spot, miles away from both the sea and the nearest big town. Mary was so distraught with the projected move that she resisted the preparations for leaving with 'much passion and weeping'. She announced bitterly that the only move she intended to make was to go into the English queen's presence. However, in the end, much to Knollys's relief, she proved 'very tractable' and made the journey on 15 July 1568 without further protest. Knollys was pleased to note that she bore no grudge against him: 'she hath that good nature that although she cannot forbear to utter her stomach, so yet she is soon pacified again, or rather she will seek reconciliation in pleasant sort and manner'.[68]

Although she continued to be heavily guarded, Mary was actually far more comfortable at Bolton. Elizabeth provided her with some geldings, and she was permitted to hunt in the royal parks and chases. The castle itself was centrally heated, and came to be well furnished after the northern lords and gentry provided furniture, tapestries and Turkish rugs for her use. Elizabeth herself loaned some pewter vessels, as well as a copper kettle. By September 1568, Mary's household had expanded to almost 140 people, and she enjoyed the presence of those loyal members of her staff who had joined her from Scotland. During the summer months she was permitted to see and entertain English visitors without interference, although care was taken that she was never left alone with them or out of Knollys's earshot. Despite this relatively good treatment, Mary was understandably frustrated by her captivity. She repeatedly pleaded with Elizabeth to give her an audience and, desperate to win the queen's good opinion, she agreed to accept a Protestant chaplain and hear services according to the Book of Common Prayer.

Elizabeth, however, was not to be moved. Instead of agreeing to see Mary or set her free, she offered to mediate between the deposed queen and the Confederate Lords. Elizabeth's plan was to set up a tribunal that would inquire into the reasons behind the lords' rebellion and then judge the validity of the accusations of adultery and murder they levelled against Mary. If Mary were found innocent, she could return to Scotland as

Letter from Sir Francis Knollys to Elizabeth, dated 30 May 1568 'at night'. In the earlier part of the letter (not shown) he details a conversation he had with Mary in which he spoke of the right of subjects to depose their princes lawfully in certain cases. Quite typically, Mary became distressed and shed tears, a reaction that led Knollys to react chivalrously. Halfway down he writes:

'This far I waded with her grace to make her cause disputable, but when I saw her tears I forbore to prosecute mine objection, and fell to comforting of her with declaration of your highness's great affection and good will towards her.'

(British Library, Cotton Caligula C 1, f. 114v)

Report by Knollys on
Mary's demeanour at
Carlisle, dated 11 June 1568.
Although a staunch
Protestant with no liking
for the Scottish queen,
Knollys gives a favourable
report of her, writing in the
second paragraph:

'And yet this lady and
princess is a notable
woman. She seemeth to
regard no ceremonious
honour besides the
acknowledging of her
estate regal. She showeth a
disposition to speak much,
to be bold, to be pleasant
and to be very familiar. She
showeth a great desire to
be avenged of her enemies,
she showeth a readiness to
expose herself to all perils
in hope of victory.'

(British Library, Cotton
Caligula C I, f. 124)

titular queen, but with limitations on her power. If not, she would remain a prisoner in England. This form of judicial process suited Elizabeth as it ostensibly avoided putting Mary on trial, a procedure that was unacceptable to both queens; they both believed that an anointed sovereign like Mary was accountable to God alone, and certainly not to a neighbouring ruler. Elizabeth was not to be persuaded by Cecil that she had the right to try Mary on the historically dubious grounds that the English monarch had lordship over Scotland in the island of Britain.

During the summer of 1568 English diplomats successfully persuaded both Moray and Mary to send representatives to put their case before Elizabeth's tribunal. Mary acquiesced in this process because she thought it would result in her restoration, while Moray agreed because Cecil had assured him that Mary would not be acquitted and released. Elizabeth and Cecil clearly had different objectives: the queen wanted Mary to return to Scotland as nominal sovereign while leaving Moray at the head of the government; her principal secretary wanted to see Mary discredited, condemned and placed in prison within England. Cecil had a less elevated view of monarchy than his mistress, and put the interests of his religion before the rights of anointed sovereigns. He consequently used all his influence to put before Elizabeth strong arguments against Mary's reinstatement.

In preparation for the tribunal, the Scottish Confederate Lords put together a body of

ABOVE AND OPPOSITE
Cecil's notes for and against the Queen of Scots, dated 20 June 1568. In order to appear impartial, Cecil wrote down arguments both for and against Mary, but it is clear from the weight of his arguments that he saw her as a danger and wanted her to remain in custody in England. Amongst the points in her favour, he includes: she came into England 'willingly', trusting that Elizabeth would help her; she had not been legally condemned for the murder of her husband; 'she is a Queen and monarch. Subject to none'; and she alleged 'great matters' against her rebel subjects. On the opposing side, Cecil maintains: she procured the murdering of her husband, who was a king, so their subjects were

honour bound to punish
the offenders; she
protected Bothwell and
procured his acquittal; 'she
also procured him to be
divorced from his lawful
wife'; 'she after this fained
herself to be forcibly taken
by him and carried away';
she afterwards married
'this principal murderer'
and gave him great estates.
(British Library, Cotton
Caligula C I, ff. 139r, 139v)

evidence against Mary. The author of their report (known as the Book of Articles) was George Buchanan, who had once been the Scottish queen's tutor and courtier, but had then joined the rebels in the belief that she had murdered Darnley. His report was supported by eight incriminating letters and a sequence of twelve sonnets, all supposedly written in Mary's own hand to Bothwell. These were the famous 'Casket Letters' that it was claimed George Dalgliesh had handed over to Morton the previous summer in a silver casket. Most of the letters were billets-doux allegedly written by Mary to Bothwell while she had been married to Darnley, and thus provided evidence of her adultery; but one of them (known as the 'Long Glasgow' letter because it was purportedly written to Bothwell from Glasgow) also appeared to implicate Mary directly in Darnley's murder. Since the original manuscripts disappeared in the 1580s, scholars cannot now subject the letters to scrutiny, but have to work instead on French transcriptions and the English and Scottish translations that were made at the time. As a result, they have debated long and inconclusively on the authenticity of these Casket Letters. Even today historians cannot agree whether or not they were written by Mary and incriminate her in adultery with Bothwell and Darnley's murder. Although Morton and Moray clearly had a motive to fabricate the letters, a number of historians doubt that they had the time or the expertise to produce forgeries. But did they doctor the texts to make Mary's own innocent letters and sonnets appear suspicious?

Mary's Arrival in England

ABOVE

Final page of a letter from Mary to Elizabeth, dated 17 May 1568. Written from Workington, this is the first letter Mary wrote after arriving in England. In the main part of its six pages Mary writes of the treasonable proceedings of her subjects and entreats Elizabeth to see her as soon as possible:

'...for I am in a pitiable condition not only for a queen but for a gentlewoman for I have nothing in the world but what I had on my person when I made my escape travelling sixty miles across the country the first day and not having since ever ventured to proceed except by night.'

She signs herself 'Your very faithful, affectionate, good sister and cousin and an escaped prisoner'.
(British Library, Cotton Caligula C I, f. 94v)

OPPOSITE

First page of a letter from Mary to Elizabeth, dated 28 May 1568 and written from Carlisle. Mary has received two letters from 'her good sister' and hopes to be able to answer one of them 'by word of mouth' rather than by letter. She has heard from Lord Scrope and Elizabeth's vice-chamberlain (Knollys) of 'votre naturelle et votre bonne inclination en vers moi' (your natural and good inclination towards me) and hopes her affection for Elizabeth is also apparent. Apart from exchanging words of affection, the letter is concerned to obtain Elizabeth's permission for Mary to come before her and plead her cause.
(British Library, Cotton Caligula CI, f. 75)

Ma Dame ma bonne sœur i'ay resceu deus de vos
letters a la premiere desquelles i'espere fayre respo[n]=
de bousche moy mesmes & par milord scrup e[t] votre
vischamerlan entandu votre naturelle bonne inclin[ation]
on vers moy ce que en certitude ie me suis tousiou[r]
promis & vouldroys que mon affection vers vous
vous feut aussi aparante que sans fiction ie la
vous porte 'nenixe & alors vous panceries vo[stre]
bonne voulontay mieulx emploiee que ie ne vo[us]
scauroys persnader par mes humbles merc[is]
madame ie suis marrie que la haste en laque[lle]
ie conius ma dernière lettre ma fayt obmettre
comme i'apercoys par la votre la prinsipalle
chose qui me meut a la vous escrire & qui[...]
est ast cause prinsiple de ma venue en ce
votre royaulme qui est qu'ayant ce long temp
estay prisonière & comme desiaie vous auoys ec[...]
tretée iniustement tant par leur fayts q[...]pa[...]
leur faulx raports ie desiroys sur tout venir
personne vous fayre ma complaynte tant pou[r]
la proximite de sang de similytude d'estat[...]
professee amitie que pour me descharger

Several historians (most recently John Guy) argue that this is exactly what happened: either additional material from other letters was interpolated into the texts, or else innocent letters were presented out of context or wrongly dated. We can never be entirely certain, but I am inclined to accept the arguments of those who question the authenticity of the letters and consequently the evidence for Mary's guilt.

Elizabeth's tribunal opened at York on 4 October 1568. The judges she appointed were Thomas Howard, the 4th Duke of Norfolk (the most senior peer of the realm), Thomas Radcliffe, the 3rd Earl of Sussex (Howard's cousin, who had been recently appointed president of the Council of the North), and Sir Ralph Sadler (who was rightly considered an expert in Scottish affairs). After the official preliminaries, Mary's team produced her formal complaint against Moray and the Confederate Lords, who in response justified their rebellion on the grounds of Mary's marriage to Bothwell. At this juncture, Moray said that he had evidence of Mary's complicity in Darnley's murder, but that he could not make formal charges or produce the documents unless, and until, Elizabeth promised to support his government and abandon Mary if his case were proved. This guarantee Elizabeth was not yet prepared to make. So to give herself more time to think about her options, she decided to adjourn the inquiry and reconvene it later in London.

While at York, the English judges were shown the Casket Letters 'privately and secretly'.

Ane Detectioun of the Duings of Marie, Quene of Scottes, Touchand the Murder of Hir Husband... by George Buchanan (1571). This book includes an account of the Casket Letters (letters and sonnets allegedly written by Mary, and that purportedly prove her adultery with Bothwell and guilt in the plot to murder Darnley). (British Library, C55.a.26)

on amour & ferme affection.
eſt il pas ia en poſſeſsion
orps, du cœur qui ne refuſe paine
eſhonneur, en la vie incertaine,
nſe de parentz, ne pire affliction?
luy tous mes amis i' eſtime moins que rien,
iazardé pour luy & nom & conſcience:
ux pour luy au monde renoncer:
ux mourir pour luy auancer.
reſte il plus pour prouuer ma conſtance?

e ſes mains & en ſon plein pouuoir
tz mon filz, mon honneur, & ma vie,
païs, mes ſubiectz, mon ame aſſubiectie
ut à luy, & n' ay autre voulloir
mon obiect que ſans le deceuoir
e ie veux malgré toute l' enuie
ſir en peult, Car ie n' ay autre enuie
le ma foy, luy faire apperceuoir
pour tempeſte ou bonnace qui face
s ne veux changer demeure ou place.
ie feray de ma foy telle preuue,
cognoiſtra ſans fainte ma conſtance,
ar mes pleurs ou fainte obeyſſance,
ne autres ont fait, mais par diuers eſpreuue.

our ſon honneur vous doibt obeyſſance
vous obeyſſant i' en puis receuoir blaſme,

While Norfolk appeared to be shocked by some of them, especially the 'Long Glasgow' letter, Sussex was less inclined to accept their genuineness, and was certainly not convinced that they would result in Mary's condemnation if produced in a court of law. Mary, he recognized, would not only reject the documents as forgeries, but could also, with justice, accuse the Confederate Lords of complicity in Darnley's murder. Yet despite the difficulty of finding evidence to convict Mary, Sussex did not advise that she should be set free or returned to Scotland: as he told Cecil, 'I think surely no end can be made good for England except that the person of the Scotch Queen be detained, by one means or other, in England'.[69] Cecil, of course, needed no persuading on this point.

On Thursday 25 November 1568 an enlarged tribunal met in the Painted Chamber at Westminster, London, to resume the proceedings started at York. By this time the Privy Council had convinced a reluctant Elizabeth that Moray had to be given the guarantees he sought so that he would present his proofs of Mary's guilt. Otherwise, Elizabeth would have no justification for holding her cousin under restraint or refusing her aid. Once Moray's evidence was admitted, Mary's representatives – principally John Leslie, the Bishop of Ross, and Lord Herries – demanded that their queen be permitted to attend the tribunal and answer his accusations in person. When Elizabeth refused, they withdrew in protest. Thereupon Moray was given a clear run to present his case against Mary and

First Trial of Mary

ABOVE LEFT

Portrait of Sir William Cecil, later Lord Burghley, c.1560–70 by Arnold von Bronckhorst. Elizabeth's principal secretary until 1572, Cecil wanted Mary to be put on trial in 1568. (National Portrait Gallery, London)

ABOVE RIGHT

Cecil's justification for putting Mary on trial, May 1568. Amongst his notes on Mary, point three asserts English jurisdiction over Scotland – a claim Cecil makes so that Mary can be put on trial in England for the murder of her husband.

'Note that it appeareth honourable and meet for the Q. Majesty as Queen of England to take upon her the hearing, deciding and determining of any controversy moved for the crown of Scotland; for that of ancient right it appertaineth to the Crown of England as by multitude of records, examples, and precedents may be proved.'

(British Library, Cotton Caligula C. I, f. 98)

OPPOSITE

Letter from Elizabeth to Mary, dated 21 December 1568. Written at the end of the first trial of Mary, this letter blames the Scottish queen for the conclusion of the judicial inquiry that began at York and ended at Hampton Court. Mary had demanded to attend in person to respond to the Scottish rebels' charges against her, and commanded her representatives to make no answer. Without hearing Mary's side of the story, Elizabeth was unable to decide whether or not the rebels were justified in their rebellion and could make no final judgment. Seven lines down from the top she writes:

'...as we have been very sorry of long time for your mishaps and great troubles, so find we our sorrows now doubled in beholding such things [the Casket Letters] as are produced to prove your self cause of all the same. And our grief herein is also increased in that we did not think at any time to have seen or heard such matter of great appearance and moment to charge and condemn you. Nevertheless both in friendship, nature and justice, we are moved to cover these matters and stay our judgment...before we may hear of your direct answer.'

Towards the end of the letter, Elizabeth commends the Bishop of Ross 'who not only faithfully and wisely, but also so carefully and dutifully, for your honour and weal behaved himself'. Because of her good opinion of Ross, Elizabeth afterwards opened direct negotiations with him for the restoration of Mary. However, his later involvement in the Ridolfi plot ended his role as intermediary between Elizabeth and Mary.
(British Library, Cotton Caligula C I, f. 367)

publicize the Casket Letters to the tribunal. After he had finished, Elizabeth summoned a wider group of councillors and nobility to Hampton Court, where they too heard the evidence against Mary. All agreed it was substantial. By this means Elizabeth won a public relations victory in demonstrating Mary's unsuitability to be Queen of England, let alone of Scotland. However, without Mary's response to the charges, no judgment of guilt (or indeed innocence) could be made and, consequently, Elizabeth was no nearer solving the problem of Mary's future.

Behind the scenes, Elizabeth tried to persuade Mary to answer Moray's charges in writing or through commissioners so that a final judgment could be reached. Mary, however, utterly refused, and demanded her right to face her accusers in person: 'to answer otherwise than in person before your presence, she sayeth she never meant,' Knollys informed Elizabeth.[70] Elizabeth then tried to reach a private settlement, whereby Mary would hand over her crown to her son and live voluntarily in England. Mary would have none of it. By the end of the year Elizabeth had decided nothing more could be done, and on 10 January 1569 she brought the judicial hearing to an inconclusive end. The case against Mary was declared to be not proven; no verdict could be arrived at 'till she hear further of the Queen of Scotland's answers to such things as have been alleged against her'.[71] In the meantime, Mary would be held in England, while Moray was sent home to govern Scotland with a £5,000 English loan.

While Mary was at Bolton awaiting the outcome of the tribunal held at York, her custodians grew fearful that their 'guest' might attempt an escape. They were aware that some English Catholics had gained access to Mary, and they heard rumours that plans were being hatched to set her free. In fact, Mary was prepared to sit out her detention and await the judgment of Elizabeth's tribunal, for she was hopeful of a positive outcome. Her English companion, Lady Scrope, had assured her that Norfolk would be a sympathetic judge in her cause, and that Sussex would follow his lead. Ignorant of this, Knollys warned Elizabeth of a possible attempt at a getaway, and advised that the security at Bolton needed improvement. In response, Elizabeth took measures to cut off Mary from potential sympathizers and escape routes. In September 1568 Lady Scrope was told to leave the castle and take up lodgings two miles away. The following month Elizabeth ordered that the number of English visitors to the castle should be restricted. Soon afterwards, she dismissed Mary's Scottish horsemen and told Scrope and Knollys to accompany Mary every time she went outside. When they objected that they could not keep Mary under such 'restraint' without turning her into a prisoner, Elizabeth showed little sympathy: 'we would have her so kept and ordered as neither she should escape nor yet be reported to be a prisoner'.[72]

As the proceedings of the tribunal drew to a close, it became obvious that Mary's stay in England would be prolonged. Arrangements were consequently put in place to consign her

Portrait of Elizabeth Talbot,
Countess of Shrewsbury,
c.1590 by an unknown
artist. Bess of Hardwick,
as she is better known,
was Mary's custodian
and companion while the
Scottish queen resided at
the Earl of Shrewsbury's
properties in Staffordshire
and Derbyshire. Eventually,
Bess quarrelled with her
charge.
(National Portrait Gallery,
London)

to a stronghold even further from the border, far away from possible sympathizers in the Catholic-inclined North, and some distance from any seaport. The location chosen was the motte and bailey castle at Tutbury, near Burton upon Trent in Staffordshire. New custodians were also appointed: the lessees of the castle, George Talbot, the 6th Earl of Shrewsbury, and his second wife, Elizabeth, who is better known today as Bess of Hardwick.

Mary began the move to Tutbury in late January 1569. Moving slowly in the depth of winter, the journey took eight days and she arrived at the castle on 3 February. Her new accommodation was far less comfortable than Bolton had been. 'I am in a walled enclosure, on the top of a hill exposed to the winds and inclemencies of heaven,' she complained, and her own apartments were 'two little miserable rooms, so excessively cold, especially at night'.[73] Her household was also smaller; initially it comprised sixty attendants, but was soon cut to thirty, excluding women and grooms of the stable. Even before their arrival, Shrewsbury was concerned about the lack of comfort, and wrote to Elizabeth requesting extra furnishings to be sent from the Tower of London. But these could not greatly improve the living quarters, which remained bleak and damp. Parts of the building were in ruins or 'indifferently well repaired'; even worse, the castle overlooked a large marsh with unpleasant fumes. In this place Mary's health began to deteriorate rapidly, and she developed rheumatism, a persistent fever and 'grief of the spleen'.[74] Worried about her condition,

Norfolk, His Marriage Scheme and the Ridolfi Plot

Portrait of Thomas Howard, 4th Duke of Norfolk,
1563 by Hans Eworth. Howard was the leading judge
at the hearing held at York in the autumn of 1568
that inquired into the reasons for the Scottish lords'
rebellion against Mary. Soon afterwards he entered
into secret negotiations to marry her.
(Private collection)

Norfolk's submission to the queen, 23 June
1570, 'whereupon he was delivered out of the Tower
and remitted to his house at Charterhouse'. Norfolk
was sent to the Tower of London for discussing a
marriage to Mary without first obtaining Elizabeth's
permission. Here he acknowledges his 'offence' and
offers to make amends 'with a determined mind
never to offend your majesty either in the same or
any like. Beseeching your most gracious goodness
to accept me into your favour'. In the second
paragraph Norfolk writes:

'And where I did unhappily give ear to certain motions made to me in a cause of marriage to be prosecuted for me with the Queen of Scots, I most humbly beseech your majesty to permit me to declare such part of the truth that maketh in some part my excuse.'

His excuses were that he never intended to harm his queen and that he always meant to bring the matter before her for approval or disapproval. But he admits that 'I did err very much in that I did not cause the same to be known to your majesty upon the first motion made to me.'
(British Library, Additional MS 48023, f. 147)

ABOVE
The 'principal causes showed against the Queen of Scots by the Queen's Majesty's learned council', [1572]. Here are listed the details of the Ridolfi plot: Mary's long letter in cipher to the Bishop of Ross, in which she shows that she 'resteth at the last upon Spain', and her communications with Philip II and the pope.

'The going of Ridolfi accordingly first to the D[uke] of Alva, then to the Pope, and after to Sp[ain] with instructions: whereunto were privy the D[uke] of Norfolk, the Sp[anish] Amb[assado]r, and B[ishop] of Ross.'

Ridolfi's message was 'to procure 1000 men to arrive in England and to join with the Duke and his friends'. Alva accepted the request, and Ridolfi wrote in cipher to the other conspirators. The pope wrote to Mary and to the duke. 'The B[ishop] of Ross hath confessed all this and the whole practices in a letter which he sent to the Q[ueen] of Scots since he was in the Tower.'

Also mentioned were 'Her practices with Rolleston, Hall, Sir Thomas Stanley and Sir Thomas Gerard for her escape by force'; and finally George Rolleston's confession that he intended 'to proclaim them [Norfolk and Mary] King and Queen of England'.
(British Library, Additional MS 48049, f. 250)

Shrewsbury asked if she could be moved to one of his more attractive residences, so Elizabeth gave permission for her transfer to Wingfield Manor, ten miles from Chesterfield in Derbyshire, where she arrived on 20 April 1569. Although Wingfield was a more pleasant environment, Mary's health still did not improve. She therefore went to stay at Bess's well-situated new house at Chatsworth in Derbyshire, where she rode, hawked, practised archery and rested in the parks and gardens during the summer months. There was little opportunity for escape from the house, as it was situated in moorland and distant from any town.

While at Wingfield and Chatsworth Mary was given a great deal more freedom. In part, this was because Shrewsbury was unwell, and security began to grow lax. Mary's friends were permitted greater access to her, as was a disguised Catholic priest. Additionally, Mary smuggled out letters to Philip II and the Duke of Alva, Philip's governor-general in the Netherlands. A little later, she began a secret romantic correspondence with the Duke of Norfolk in which they discussed marriage. The idea of such a marriage had been mooted with Norfolk the previous autumn while he sat on the tribunal at York. Maitland of Lethington, then one of Moray's supporters, had first suggested it, and afterwards Mary's adherent the Bishop of Ross also raised the possibility. Before leaving for Scotland, Moray spoke with the duke about a marriage, and even promised to give it his support provided that Elizabeth gave her consent.

For Norfolk, the match was an attractive proposition, despite the evidence of the Casket Letters, which had so horrified him when first viewed. A marriage into royalty, even for England's premier peer, could only enhance his status and add to his political power. Furthermore, Norfolk could argue that the match was very much in the national interest, for it would resolve the decade-long succession issue and the more recent problem about what to do with the Scottish queen. According to his thinking, with a Protestant English husband by her side, Mary could be trusted to be officially named Elizabeth's heir and safely reinstated on the Scottish throne. For her part, Mary saw in Norfolk a route to freedom. Remembering how Elizabeth had pressed the suit of Leicester some four years earlier as part of a political settlement, Mary apparently expected Elizabeth to approve again her marriage to a loyal Englishman and, after it took place, to work actively for her restoration to the Scottish throne. Both Norfolk and Mary badly miscalculated. In the first place, Elizabeth could hardly take kindly to a marriage negotiated behind her back, and would naturally suspect the loyalty of all those involved. Second, Moray and his allies would under no circumstances agree to Mary's restoration; the regent had only offered to support the Norfolk marriage in the belief that Elizabeth would never permit it. Moray's position became perfectly clear after the end of the conference at Westminster, when he and his allies foiled Elizabeth's attempts to negotiate Mary's reinstatement. In early August 1569 a convention of the Scottish lords rejected the idea of Mary's return by forty votes to nine.

Nonetheless, the Mary–Norfolk marriage project soon won the backing of a group of noblemen and politicians at Elizabeth's court. Leicester, Pembroke, Throckmorton and Arundel all approved the scheme, though predictably Cecil, who learnt of it some time later (in mid-July), was quietly hostile. Agreeing to act as marriage brokers, Leicester and Pembroke formally proposed the match to Mary, setting down in a letter the conditions she would have to accept to allow it to go ahead: the continuation of Protestantism in Scotland, and an Anglo-Scottish league of friendship. Mary, of course, agreed. She and Norfolk exchanged love tokens as a sign of their commitment; he sent her a diamond and, in return, she sent him a miniature of herself set in gold. No one, however, dared to broach the matter with Elizabeth, but, in the hothouse atmosphere of the court, the negotiations could not be kept secret for long. As early as December 1568 Elizabeth had tackled Norfolk about rumours she had heard concerning the match, but he had hotly denied them, claiming that he had no thoughts of marrying such a notorious adulteress and murderer: 'I love to sleep upon a safe pillow,' he told her reassuringly, if misleadingly.[75] In August 1569 news of the marriage scheme again reached Elizabeth's ears, and she tried to prod the duke into admitting all he knew. Norfolk, though, said nothing. Aware that she was being deceived, Elizabeth lost her temper and angrily rounded upon both Leicester and Norfolk.

Leicester soon revealed all to the queen and begged her forgiveness, but Norfolk declined to apologize, and instead truculently stood his ground, defending the marriage as a sensible policy. Understandably furious, Elizabeth commanded him to give up any such ideas.

Norfolk then behaved even more foolishly. Fearing punishment, he took fright and left the court without permission, shortly afterwards bolting to his country seat at Kenninghall in East Anglia. Elizabeth was thoroughly alarmed. In the belief that the duke and his friends planned to raise the country on behalf of Mary, she took immediate precautions. Norfolk was sent to the Tower on 11 October, while the Earl of Huntingdon was dispatched to join Shrewsbury in keeping watch over Mary and to supervise her removal to more secure accommodation. Armed men searched Mary's rooms at Wingfield, and she was then sent back to Tutbury. Her quarters there were even worse than they had been earlier in the year when she had fallen ill, for she was placed in rooms overlooking the castle's sewers, and her rooms stank as the privies were emptied beneath her window. To add to this, her retinue was reduced and her communication with the outside world cut off. Not surprisingly, Mary hated Tutbury, but she was not to stay there long, for in the last week of November 1569 she was removed to the Midlands. In that month the Catholic earls of Northumberland and Westmorland called out the North in an armed rising, with the intention of liberating Mary and returning England to the Catholic religion. In case a group of rebels made for Tutbury, Huntingdon was ordered to take Mary further south, to the castle at Coventry. When they arrived, however, the castle was found to be uninhabitable, so Mary had to be lodged first at an inn and then in a private house within the walls of the town. She stayed at Coventry for two months in virtual isolation, before returning to Tutbury once the immediate danger was over. Then, in May 1570, she revisited Chatsworth, where she was free to ride, hunt and hawk in the park.

During 1570 Elizabeth again attempted to negotiate the return of Mary to Scotland. Discussions were reopened with the Bishop of Ross, and in October Cecil and Sir Walter Mildmay went to Chatsworth to confer with Mary about a settlement, while representatives of the regent's party were summoned to London. Events within both Scotland and France had prompted these initiatives. At the beginning of the year, Regent Moray had been assassinated, and Scotland descended into civil war as leading figures (notably Maitland of Lethington and Kirkcaldy of Grange) defected to Mary's party. Although stability was somewhat restored in July with the election of a new regent (Mary's father-in-law, Lennox), the civil war lingered on. The political situation in France had also changed. In 1570 Charles IX managed to restore order over his realm, which for most of the 1560s had been in the throes of civil war, and, as a result, the French were at last in a position to re-establish their connections in Scotland and offer military support to the Marians. Faced with this threat, Elizabeth tried to head Charles off

by restarting negotiations for Mary's restoration. Once again, though, the Scottish lords in charge of the government proved uncooperative, and the talks went nowhere.

Meanwhile, during the summer of 1570, an escape plot was devised by some English Catholic gentlemen: Sir Thomas Gerard, the brothers Francis and George Rolleston, and two younger sons of the Earl of Derby, Sir Thomas and Sir Edward Stanley. Their plan was thoroughly amateurish and ill conceived. Although the plotters aimed to rescue Mary while she was out hunting, they had no clear idea about what to do next: how to get her undetected to a port, and whether to put her on a boat for the Continent, Scotland or the

OPPOSITE

Letter from the Bishop of Ross to Cecil, dated 8 July 1570. Here, as part of the negotiations for Mary's restoration, the bishop tells Cecil that he would have liked them to have met to discuss Mary's affairs, but 'seeing the commodity of meeting can not serve', he is writing this letter to assure the secretary that 'the Queen my mistress's intentions and mind is wholly bent to satisfy' them in the matter of the security of Elizabeth and 'this your native country'. Ross pledges in line eleven:

'...to that end she will leave no thing undone that lieth in her possibility, yea and neither for pleasure of any other prince nor for alteration of religion, will she give any occasion of offence to her majesty'.

He goes on to say that she will procure all other princes who are her friends to concur. A league between the monarchs of England, Scotland and France might follow. (British Library, Cotton Caligula C II, f. 31)

Please your honor, your last letter being received giveth me occasion to think, that your honor conceaved some opinion of our dealings, otherwayes then we do meane, or put you in hope of, at my last coming. And therfore, to avoyde any scruple may occur, and to winne your reply, I wold have bene very glade, to have conferred with your honor, but saying the commoditie of meeting can not serve, and that it is perillous, to suffer any suspicion or mistrust to take roote, I have thought nedefull to make this letter, to assure your honor, that he knoweth my most true intentions and mynd, is wholy bent to satisfie these two pointes, wherof I perswade you as most carefull, not the first the safety of the state of law & matter sovereigne, and thus your preservation. And to that end, she will take no time unknowne that by the power possibilitie yea and neither by persuasion of any other prince or by alteration of religion, will she give any occasions of offence to be made, but will altogether joyne her self for defence of the crown, your sovereigne estate and of this her entries, against whosoever will attempt to invade the same. And will procure by all meanes possible, to procure all other princes, her neighbour frendes, to contrer and joynes with her for that effect. And speciallie the king of France, in respect he doth interpone him self presentlie for her reliefe. And therupon I have considered with my self, that yf the king be myght be brought to be oblist in the like conditions with the crown mate your sovereigne and her crown my most, that they all three myght be joyned in a league defensive to take au faite of other wise other of France there, whatsoever that wold procure to invade, any of their realmes or dominions, under whatsoever collour inclose. In that case I think her wold be strong ynough. And thought well all jolofiest mistrusty dealing afterwards, either by the crown may beginning, or the said king, wold be taken away. Wherof you possibly I have alreadie opened to this ambassador, who likethe well therof and hopes that the king his said master, myght be made agreeable to the same. I pray your honor conferre of this, and breake it to the crown mate yf that by some findes it good. And yf yow shall think this, or any other course may serve for her majesty sovereigne, let me knowe therof that her crown my most, and I her simplest minister shall dispose our selves reply to further the same. So remitting to your care. In the meanetyme I commit your honor most to the protection of god eternall. From Lundone this yesterday at noone the last day this July 15...

your honor assured to command

Jo. ...

Letter allegedly from Mary to Norfolk, written in cipher. According to the decoded transcript, Mary expresses concern about Norfolk's health, and her fears about the practices of her enemies, especially the regent. She hopes that 'if Leicester and Pembroke be your friends', they can counterbalance the influence of Moray. She ends by assuring Norfolk of his constancy:

'Last of all I pray you my good lord trust none that shall say that I ever mind to leave you... I remain yours till death.'

(British Library, Cotton Caligula C II, f. 69)

Isle of Man. Some of the conspirators met with Mary's steward on the Derbyshire moors above Chatsworth, and they exchanged a cipher so that they could maintain a secret correspondence with the Scottish queen. But, although desperate to escape, Mary showed no inclination 'to adventure upon a mere uncertainty'[76] and kept her distance from the conspirators, preferring to put her trust in the negotiations with Elizabeth. It was a wise decision. The plot was betrayed in late 1570, and all the conspirators were arrested, though let off with a severe warning. Despite this, Chatsworth was considered unsafe, and in late November 1570 Mary was moved to the heavily fortified Sheffield Castle, at the confluence of the rivers Don and Sheaf. Sheffield Castle and the adjoining manor, a couple of miles away, were to be Mary's main residences for the next fourteen years, with only short breaks away in Buxton, Chatsworth and Worksop Manor.

Mary had not been at Sheffield Castle long when she became involved in a new and far more serious plot. This one was not planned by a few madcap Catholic gentlemen, but had the backing of Norfolk, Philip II of Spain, the pope, the Bishop of Ross and two other English noblemen, the Earl of Arundel and Lord Lumley. Its instigator was Roberto Ridolfi, a Florentine banker resident in London, whom many historians believe was a double agent working for the English government. Ridolfi dreamed up an ambitious, not to say unrealistic, scheme that involved the rescue of Mary, the capture of Elizabeth, the incitement of a Catholic rising and a Spanish invasion of eastern England from the Low Countries. The objective was, therefore, not just to free Mary but to marry her to Norfolk and place them both on the English throne. By the late summer of 1571, the English government had fairly easily broken the code used by Ridolfi and uncovered full details of the plot. The Bishop of Ross and Norfolk were immediately arrested. Threatened with torture, the bishop made a detailed confession that admitted his mistress's involvement in Ridolfi's nefarious schemes and contained all sorts of wild accusations.

How much Norfolk and Mary knew about the overall purpose of Ridolfi's plot is uncertain. Both of them, however, were undeniably carrying out secret negotiations with the banker: Norfolk met Ridolfi soon after he had been released from the Tower in August 1570, and even if the duke did not agree to instigate a Catholic rising (after all, he was a Protestant), he was drawn into a scheme to free and marry Mary, despite his promise to Elizabeth that he would 'never deal in the matter again nor in any cause concerning her [the Scottish queen]'.[77] He also sold off his family silver and jewels to finance an army, and forwarded money to the Marians in Scotland; and he made contact with the Spanish ambassador in England and other disaffected Catholic nobles. Therefore, although he pleaded innocence in a plot to assassinate the queen, he was clearly dabbling in treason. As for Mary, she had written letters to Norfolk, Philip II and the pope asking for assistance, and she had been in communication with Ridolfi. The exact

Tutbury Imprisonment

Portrait of George Talbot, 6th Earl of Shrewsbury, c.1580 by an unknown artist. Talbot was Mary's long-serving custodian at Tutbury and elsewhere.
(National Portrait Gallery, London)

A list of items sent to Tutbury for Mary's use, 20 January 1569. The bleak and half-ruined castle of Tutbury in Staffordshire was appointed a new residence for Mary. To make it a little more comfortable, the Earl of Shrewsbury asked for furnishings to be sent from the Tower of London. As seen here, they included hangings, tapestries, Turkish carpets, four beds and bolsters, three chairs, eight cushions of cloth of gold, low stools and footstools, sheets and pillowcases.
(British Library, Additional MS 33593, f. 15)

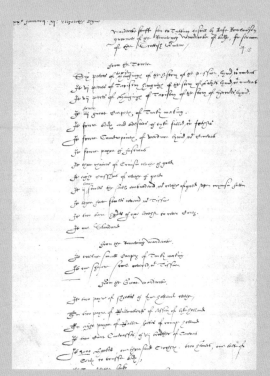

Letter from Mary to Elizabeth, dated 1 October 1569. Written at Tutbury, where Mary was sent after the discovery of her correspondence with Norfolk, this is a formal letter (written in the hand of her secretary). As always, Mary addresses Elizabeth as '_ma bonne soeur_' (my good sister), since in her eyes they were sister monarchs. She begins by complaining that Elizabeth has reached no favourable resolution about her case as had been promised and that she is kept a prisoner:

'I have only been able to lament that my confidence in you, and my friendship and desire to please you have brought me a result so unhoped for and evil in recompense for my long forbearance.'

She goes on to protest at the _rigueur_ (severity) of the conditions in which she now lives. She has had to dismiss some of her servants, can receive no letters or messages, and is unable to deal with her affairs in Scotland 'that are in such extremity', or to hear from her friends or relations in France. She has been prevented from going outside, and the chests in her chamber have been searched by guards 'with pistols and arms, not without putting me in bodily fear'. She is sending the Bishop of Ross to Elizabeth with letters protesting her innocence, and begs Elizabeth to effect her restoration or allow her to retire to France. If Elizabeth desires to detain her as a prisoner, she asks to be ransomed. The letter is signed 'your very affectionate, distressed sister and cousin'.
(British Library, Cotton Caligula C I, f. 325)

...manier que ma fiance en vous, mon amitiay & desir de vous complaire mayent aporté
si inesperee & mauuaise conclusion, pour recompance de ma longue pasciance: a quoy toutes
fois pancant remedier par vous resmonstrer ma sincere intantion en toutes mes actions vers vous
i aurois requis vous pouuoir eecrire par ung de mes fidelles seruiteurs esperant que congnoissan
mon inoscance vous museries autremant. mays cela me fut refusay, qui ma fait hasarder
demuoier vers lesuesque de rosse. pour lui donner ceste charge. mays ce pandant voiant la
rigueur augmanter iusques a me contreindre de chasser mes pauures seruiteurs sans leur done
permission daller ou pour mon respect ilz pourroyent auuoir leur vie, ains les forcer de ce
randre entre les meins de mes rebelles pour etre pandus, ne me voulant laysser que xx home
si ie ne voulois chasser mes fammes sans scauoir ou, sans argent, ou apui, si loing de leur pays &
tel temps: aquel nombre il ne mest possible etre seruie pour les respects que lesuesque de rosse
fera entandre a qui il vous playra. cela ma samblay troy plus dur que ie neusse iamays
sceu pancer de vous, & encores la deffance ma plus grenee que ie ne rescoyue lettre, ni mesaige
ni de mes affayres descosse, qui sont en telle extresmitay pour mestre atandue a votre promesse
destre en brief despeschee: ni mesmes mest il permis dantandre de celles de france ou porte-
nant des princes mes amys ou parans qui satandent comme iay fayct a votre faueur vers moy
u lieu de la quelle lon ma defandu de sortir, & mest on venu fouiller mes coffres, entrant
ueques pistollets & armes en ma chambre, non sans creinte de ma vie: & accuser mes gens,
es fouiller & retenir auuesgarde. encores cuidoisie quentout cela ne trouuant rien qui
vous importast ou pour vous des plaire, quapres, cela maporteroit meillieur tretemant.
mays voiant que ceste vie mest continuee, auecques aparance de pis, iay pancay vous fayre
ceste derniere requeste contenant ces points suiuants. premier que si vous trouues que la
eclaration de lesuesque de rosse ne vous satisfasse, me permeties de vous en satisfayre en
rsonne. segondemant quil vous playse sans plus me deceier pour respects daultrui me remetre
en mon pays & autoritay, par votre suport: ou me permetre selon mon enciene petition me retirer en
ance auuesques le roy treschrestien monsieur mon bonfrere: ou au moyngs que durant ma prison
re libertay de communiquer auuesques lesuesque de rosse & aultres necesayres affayres ministres
ur mettre ordre a mes affayres & a ces mienes affectionnees requestes vouloir fayre response par ung
s miens ou par votre lettre. & pour conclusion si il vous plest me retnir pour votre prisoniere ie vous
lie au moings me metre a ranson, sans me laysser consommer issi en larmes & regrets de resceuoir
a l dont iestois venu querir la medesine. mays si il vous plest muser de rigueur sans lauoyr deser-
moings que ie ne sois mise entre meins de personne suspecte a mes amis & parents pour dangier
faulx raports, ou pis que ie ne veulx pancer de personne. & esperant que considereres ces mienes
antations & requestes, celon consciance iustice, vos loyx votre honnheur, & satisfaction de tousles
ces chrestiens, ie priray dieu vous donner heurheuse & longue vie, & a moy meillieure part en
e bonnegrace qua mon regret ieay resis nauoyr par effect: a la que ie ie me recommanderay affection
ant pour la fin de ma prison a tutheri ce premier doctobre.

Votre tres affectionnee troublee soeur &
cousine mariaR

nature of her dealings with the banker is similarly unknown, but she strongly denied involvement in any plot to depose Elizabeth and return England to Catholicism, and she only admitted working for her liberty and restoration to her rightful throne. However, even if her denials were strictly speaking true, they were certainly disingenuous. Although careful not to sanction an assassination attempt against Elizabeth, Mary was still summoning help from foreign leaders and English Catholics whose aim was to remove Elizabeth from the throne. While Mary's primary objectives were undoubtedly to obtain foreign aid for her adherents in Scotland and to secure her own freedom from house arrest in England, she did not shrink from working with others whose plans were far more ambitious and threatening to Protestant England.

The Ridolfi plot did immense and irrevocable damage to Mary. Immediately it was discovered, Elizabeth allowed Buchanan's *Detectioun* and the Casket Letters to be published. At Norfolk's trial, the Crown's lawyers presented before the court of peers a damning account of Mary's activities since arriving in England, claiming that she had consistently made a bid for Elizabeth's throne. In the parliament of 1572, the Privy Council brought before the Lords and Commons a list of 'the principal causes' against Mary, which included her attempt to advance her title to the English throne by marriage to Norfolk, her incitement of the recent rebellion in the North, and her negotiations with Ridolfi to 'procure'

an invasion. Whatever sympathy had previously existed for Mary now vanished. Members of the 1572 parliament condemned her political conduct and moral behaviour, with many MPs calling for her execution. Before the end of the session, they passed a bill to exclude her from the succession and to make it a treasonable offence to advance her claim to the throne or discuss her marriage. Elizabeth, however, would not let the bill pass; not wanting to stand out against the strong feelings being expressed in both Houses of Parliament, she did not veto the measure, but said she would consider it further and probably proceed with it later in the year. Unsurprisingly, nothing more was heard of the bill.

Thanks to Elizabeth's protection, Mary was saved in 1572 from execution, the fate that befell Norfolk and was demanded by a fair number of MPs, but the Scottish queen could not afford to put another foot wrong. For the rest of her life she was demonized by English Protestants, who needed little excuse to press Elizabeth again for her execution. For nearly a decade there was no longer talk of Mary's return to Scotland; on the contrary, Elizabeth gave money and military support to Regent Lennox, and then, following his death, to his successors – first Mar, then Morton – enabling them to capture the Marian strongholds of Dumbarton Castle in April 1571 and Edinburgh Castle in May 1573.

So how justified were English fears surrounding Mary in 1572? Some historians have argued that they were exaggerated, even paranoid, or perhaps manufactured by Cecil and his allies for their own ends. While Mary's mere presence in England unquestionably sparked off the court conspiracy surrounding the Norfolk marriage and the rising of the northern earls, these historians point out that the Scottish queen cannot be seen as their instigator. She was made aware of the last-minute preparations for an insurrection, but sent word to Northumberland and Westmorland exhorting them not to rebel. Furthermore, the rebellion, once raised, was quickly and easily suppressed. Not only did many of the Catholic nobility (most notably the earls of Derby and Cumberland) remain loyal to the Crown, but also the number of rebels was relatively small; only some six thousand rallied to the Catholic cause in 1569 in contrast with the thirty thousand or so participants in the Pilgrimage of Grace, the Catholic rising in the North thirty-three years previously. The rebels were also starved of aid from abroad. As already seen, the French were preoccupied with their own internal problems until 1570, while Philip II decided to sit on the sidelines, certainly until the rising proved to be successful. Only Pope Pius V directly intervened: he had tried to mobilize support for Mary in 1569; in February 1570 he issued a bull excommunicating and deposing Elizabeth, but by then the rebellion had collapsed. The rebellion was certainly a mark of the government's failure to win over the Catholic North and to handle some of its most powerful noblemen, but, in fact, it had little realistic chance of success.

As for the Ridolfi plot, it hardly constituted a serious threat. Admittedly, an international conspiracy did exist, and disaffected English nobles were prepared to betray their queen, but the plot was a shambles and easily detected. On this occasion (unlike 1569) Philip II was committed to invasion, but he was restrained from hasty action by his governor-general in the Netherlands, who strongly opposed military intervention in England. Thanks to Alva's advice, Philip agreed to send troops only after Elizabeth had been assassinated or made prisoner, and a Catholic rising had brought Norfolk into power – neither of which, of course, happened.

However, this analysis comes only with hindsight. At the time, the fears of a Catholic conspiracy surrounding Mary seemed reasonable and realistic. After all, Mary had claimed Elizabeth's crown in the past. In the present she was known to be in communication with hostile foreign powers and English Catholics, calling on them for aid. Perhaps even more alarming, she had suborned a loyal English Protestant nobleman. The Casket Letters had revealed her to be 'lewd', ruthless and untrustworthy; the Bishop of Ross's confessions had implicated her in murder and intrigue. In these circumstances, it is no wonder that so many of Elizabeth's advisers viewed Mary as guilty of 'manifold and horrible crimes' in Scotland and 'wicked purposes' in England, and called for Elizabeth to follow the example of those Old Testament kings who had administered justice and punished their enemies in the name of the Lord.[78]

CHAPTER SIX

Captivity, Conspiracies and Execution
1572–1587

A FTER THE DEBACLE of the Ridolfi plot, Mary seemed to tire of conspiracy and for a time appeared relatively reconciled to her restricted life under house arrest in England. If she were plotting, she was at least more careful. In any event, her hopes of restoration to the Scottish throne ended with the appointment in October 1572 of her old enemy the Earl of Morton as the Scottish regent, and the utter defeat of her own party there the next year. Nor could she realistically expect much help from France or Spain. In April 1572 Charles IX had abandoned her cause when he signed a defensive treaty with Elizabeth that omitted any reference to the imprisoned queen. Her Guise cousins, meanwhile, were too embroiled in the renewed civil wars engulfing France after August 1572 to offer her any effective assistance, and by the end of 1574 her closest relation and strongest French supporter, the Cardinal of Lorraine, died. Philip II of Spain also took less interest in Mary's plight after the failure of the Ridolfi plot. In 1573 he patched up his quarrels with Elizabeth, and, over the next eight years, his major preoccupation lay in trying to suppress a revolt within his territories of the Low Countries that had spiralled out of control.

OPPOSITE
'Memorial Portrait' of Mary Queen of Scots, after 1603 by an unknown artist. This portrait was commissioned by Elizabeth Curle after Mary's execution. Curle was then living in Antwerp. The inscription on the right tells how Mary was imprisoned 'on account of religion' before 'the horrible sentence of decapitation' was carried out. The execution scene at Fotheringhay is shown on the left in the background. Curle attended Mary on the scaffold and is shown on the far right.
(The Blairs Museum, Aberdeen)

As the danger from Mary abated in the mid-1570s, the conditions of her captivity improved. Immediately after the Ridolfi plot a very strict regime had been imposed: the number in her household was reduced to below thirty people; she was no longer able to ride; and for fresh air and exercise she had to take walks on the roof or in the courtyard of Sheffield Castle. Meanwhile, regular inspections were carried out to ensure she was not engaged in any secret correspondence, and the movements of her servants were carefully monitored. Gradually, as time passed and the international situation appeared less threatening, the surveillance grew more relaxed. Mary was allowed to take on more servants and to receive visitors. In the summer of 1573 Elizabeth even granted Shrewsbury permission to receive Mary at his house at Chatsworth, and from there she was permitted go to the popular spa town of Buxton to take the waters as a medicinal cure. Notwithstanding this additional freedom, Mary remained a prisoner of the Talbots, who made sure a 'good number of men, continually armed, watched her day and night...so that, unless she could transform herself to a flea or a mouse, it was impossible that she should escape'.[79]

Mary's health was a recurring problem. She regularly complained of colds, digestive upsets, rheumatism, pains in her side, headaches, vomiting and fevers. Letters from her custodians tell of the long periods – weeks, sometimes months – she spent in bed or confined through pain to her chamber. Exactly what was wrong with her is unknown, although some doctors and biographers have suggested that she was suffering from porphyria, the hereditary illness that afflicted her descendant George III, causing his madness. The symptoms were in some respects similar – sudden bouts of vomiting, weakness in the limbs, and attacks of hysteria – but this diagnosis has to be tentative. Lack of exercise, intense stress, an understandable depression, and her old digestive disorders are surely sufficient to explain Mary's ill health.

Arriving at Buxton at the end of August 1573, Mary spent five weeks at the spa and took the cure daily, both drinking and bathing in the waters. The visit was a success and she was allowed to repeat the cure over other summers. During her visits, Shrewsbury took precautions to prevent her meeting local Catholics or strangers, and she had to give one hour's notice if she wanted to leave her rooms. When the spa was especially busy she was taken to Poole's Cavern or other limestone caves near the town. Despite these safety measures, she did on occasion meet several members of the nobility who were also taking the waters there, including the Earl of Leicester in 1578 and 1584. But whenever William Cecil (now Lord Burghley) visited the spa during the summer months, he was careful to avoid encountering Mary, and Elizabeth stayed away from Buxton altogether whenever she went on her summer progress, for fear of meeting her cousin or being forced to snub her. On occasion, Elizabeth grew anxious about Mary's public appearances at the spa and opportunities for communication with her subjects. On learning that Leicester intended to spend three weeks at Buxton while Mary was present, Elizabeth ordered him to stay away and have the restorative waters sent home to him in a bottle. Similarly, after hearing rumours that Mary was courting popularity by distributing alms to the poor at Buxton, Elizabeth ordered Shrewsbury to cut short her visits or keep his charge isolated. In response, the earl replied that only one poor cripple had managed to speak with Mary 'unknown to all my people who guarded the place', but he promised not to let it happen again.[80] Mary's last stay in Buxton was in 1584. A Latin verse, scratched with a diamond into the window of the hall where she stayed, is said to have been written by her, though no hard evidence for the attribution exists. It reads in translation:

> Buxton whose warm waters fame doth tell, Whom I, perchance, no more shall visit, farewell.

During this period, Mary's lifestyle was really quite pleasant. Her residences were comfortable and their furnishings luxurious; she ate in style and ordered expensive new clothes. When restrictions were lifted and her health allowed, she rode, hawked and played archery in the parks; she kept a number of pets, including caged birds, three spaniels and several other dogs; and she had her English and Scottish companions around her for comfort and entertainment. She could enjoy music and her favourite pastime

of embroidery. But still Mary chafed at her enforced seclusion, and the subject matter, mottoes and symbols incorporated into the panels that she designed and embroidered expressed her frustration at her imprisonment and nostalgia for her former life in France and Scotland. So Mary depicted herself as a wheel plunging downwards into the sea beneath, and as a sun in eclipse. Her attitude to Elizabeth can be seen in one panel showing a bird in a cage with a hawk hovering menacingly overhead, and in another depicting a large ginger cat – the red-haired Elizabeth – wearing a small gold crown, regarding a defenceless mouse – her prisoner, Mary. Despite these depictions, Mary kept her resentment and annoyance with Elizabeth under wraps. Still hoping to win her over, Mary offered the queen a variety of gifts made by her, including a skirt of crimson silk lined with crimson taffeta and embroidered with silver thread, a headdress decorated with gold lace and silver spangles, and three nightdresses.

In addition to these harmless activities, Mary spent a considerable amount of time in dictating her memoirs and writing letters to potential supporters. After her secretary died in August 1574, Claude Nau was chosen as a replacement by her cousin Henri, Duke of Guise, and uncle, the Cardinal of Lorraine. It was to Nau that Mary relayed her own account of the death of Darnley and marriage to Bothwell, as she wanted to leave her own version of these controversial events for her son and posterity. Mary was also determined that she should not be forgotten while still

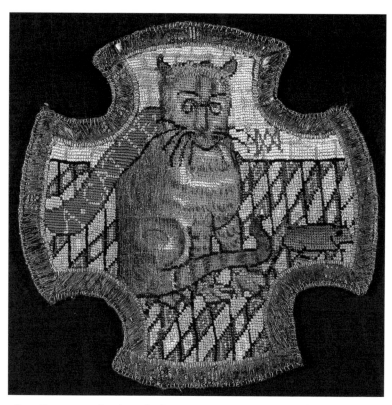

The Catte, an example of the symbolic embroidery designed and executed by Mary. In this piece the ginger cat wearing a crown represents Elizabeth, and the mouse – the object of its stare – is Mary. The Scottish queen chose her own designs from books. They were then drawn out on canvas by a succession of embroiderers, including Pierre Oudry and Charles Plouvart, who also supervised the mounting of the finished panels on to velvet.
(The Royal Collection, © 2001 Her Majesty Queen Elizabeth II)

alive. Consequently, she asked James Beaton, the Archbishop of Glasgow, who was acting as her representative in Paris, to have some miniatures made of her and distributed to loyal Catholic friends in England. On two occasions a miniaturist was secreted into Sheffield Castle – an unknown painter in 1575 and Nicholas Hilliard a few years afterwards. Throughout her captivity Mary wrote frequently to her French cousins, friends from her days in France, and some English Catholics who had sought refuge abroad. To remind them of her presence and keep their loyalty, she dispatched gifts of animals to her cousins, and granted pensions to the Catholic exiles. After 1578 she maintained a regular contact with Bernardino de Mendoza, the new

Spanish ambassador at Elizabeth's court, who claimed to have found a perfectly safe means of sending and receiving letters for her. His confidence, however, was misplaced; most of Mary's letters were intercepted, read and copied by the agents of Elizabeth's principal secretary, Sir Francis Walsingham. They convinced him that Mary was still plotting against the English queen and remained a serpent in her bosom.

Mary's enforced stay with the Talbots put considerable pressure on the earl and his wife. In the first place, Shrewsbury was forced to subsidize the cost of Mary's upkeep, which was considerable. The entertainment allowance from Elizabeth for the feeding of

*Portrait of Mary Queen of Scots, c.*1578 by Nicholas Hilliard. This miniature was probably done from life. A cross is prominently displayed around Mary's neck, and her robes are black and white, the colours she customarily wore during her captivity. Mary asked that portraits of her should be distributed amongst friends and supporters so that she would not be forgotten.
(Victoria and Albert Museum, London, UK/ Bridgeman Art Library)

the Scottish queen was usually £52 a week, but sometimes less. This sum proved to be inadequate to pay for the elaborate dinners with the many courses and expensive fare that Mary insisted upon as her right, and the earl frequently grumbled that he was out of pocket. Additionally, he had to lay out money to fund Mary's household, as well as the gentlemen and soldiers who kept watch over her. Their cost should have been covered by Mary's private income from her French dowry, but its real value dwindled, and besides, the money did not arrive regularly, so she was sometimes reduced to borrowing sums from friends and her secretary. In June 1574 Shrewsbury complained bitterly that he was obliged to spend £300 a year or more on wages, and also to pay for the soldiers to guard his unwelcome guest.

Second, the lifestyle of both the earl and Bess was circumscribed through the presence of Mary. The Talbots' contact with all outsiders was strongly discouraged: 'it seems her Majesty has no liking our children should be with us (where this Queen is),' moaned Shrewsbury.[81] When guests did arrive, they had to be vetted and searched. No one was supposed to see or speak to Mary without royal permission, and all conversations had to be carried out within earshot of Shrewsbury or his wife. Any let-up could result in a reprimand from Elizabeth, who feared that Mary would try to exercise her notorious charm to persuade visitors to help her escape, just as she had previously done at Lochleven. Indeed, any easing of the tight regime earned a rap on the knuckles, as when, in 1582, Elizabeth sent word to Shrewsbury via Burghley of her dismay on learning that 'your Lordship hath of late given her [Mary] liberty to hunt and to fish at her will', and that she had heard 'that the Queen of Scots was twice this summer at Buxton, and yet her Majesty gave licence but for one time'.[82]

Despite the inevitable strains imposed by their role as custodians, the Talbots managed for some ten years to avoid serious quarrels, both between themselves and with their unwelcome 'guest'. In 1583, however, Bess, who was then in dispute with her husband over a piece of property, suddenly accused him of carrying on an adulterous affair with Mary. Although this

accusation, almost certainly unfounded, was a weapon calculated to discredit Shrewsbury and help Bess's case, it probably brought to the surface pent-up jealousies and resentments that had been previously suppressed; after all, Mary was twenty years younger than Bess and had retained her charm and elegance, if not her good looks. When Mary found out that Bess was spreading 'scandalous reports' about her, she not only denied the stories, but also in retaliation told tales about Bess, describing her small acts of disloyalty to the queen. She put on paper details of the many times Bess had passed on unflattering gossip and mocked the queen in her presence. After this, the two women could no longer live together amicably, and Shrewsbury, who had already separated from his wife, begged to be relieved of his charge.

During her years in captivity Mary thought often of the son she had left behind in Scotland, keeping in her possession a 'book of gold enamelled' that contained his portrait. She was not, however, permitted to make contact with the Scottish king, and he made no attempt to write to her. Nevertheless, she wrote him affectionate letters and sent him a number of gifts. In July 1579 Elizabeth relented somewhat and agreed that Nau could meet with James – then a young man of thirteen – and give Mary a report on his character and appearance, but the Scots would not allow the secretary to cross the border. Later that year, however, Regent Morton fell from power, and a little later he was arrested on a charge of complicity in the murder of

James's father. The following June he was executed, and James took over the government with the help of his favourite and kinsman, the French-born Esmé Stuart, who was also a friend of Henri, Duke of Guise. This political turnabout in Scotland created an opportunity for Mary. Believing that the new government would be sympathetic to her, she put forward a proposal that she should be allowed to return home and be associated with her son as joint ruler of the realm. Using the services of her ambassador in Paris, Mary enlisted the support of the Duke of Guise to advance this project. She also wrote to Elizabeth asking for her support.

Somewhat surprisingly, Elizabeth looked on this proposal with some approval. Angry with James for turning against the anglophile Morton, and alarmed that he seemed to be listening to the advice of men who were friends of the Catholic Guises, Elizabeth decided to open talks with the Scots to see if a deal could be done that would allow Mary to go home to Scotland as co-ruler with James. She expected James and his new friends to treat Mary's release as a gesture of goodwill that would tempt them back to the English amity. But first Elizabeth needed assurances that Mary was no longer a danger to her security. For this purpose she sent her trusted clerk of the Privy Council, Robert Beale, to Sheffield in November 1581 to talk to Mary. When he arrived there, Mary was ill – or at least she claimed to be, for Beale was not entirely convinced. He therefore stayed three weeks at Sheffield before securing promises

from Mary that she would recognize Elizabeth as the legitimate Queen of England and not have any dealings with foreign rulers or English rebels.

Understandably, Mary did not trust Elizabeth, and in April 1582 – only a few months after she had given her word – she took up again her correspondence with Mendoza. One of her letters, moreover, exposed her involvement in a Spanish and papal plot to invade England and restore Catholicism there. By this time, Philip II was again looking more favourably towards Mary. Although still preoccupied with the revolt in the Low Countries, he was starting to think that his chances of suppressing it would be much enhanced if Elizabeth ceased to sit on the throne of England. Her help to his rebels had escalated in the late 1570s and early 1580s, so she was quickly becoming a serious irritant. Mendoza, meanwhile, from his base in England, was operating independently and developing conspiratorial networks with Mary, English Catholics and Jesuit missionaries.

Over the next year, little occurred to advance either Mary's plotting with Spain or negotiations with England. Elizabeth, meanwhile, used her agents in Scotland to attempt political change there that would reduce the influence of James's pro-French advisers. Basically unsuccessful, she tried again in 1583 to reach a settlement with Mary that would allow her to return home. In April Beale returned to Sheffield, where he extracted from Mary several promises. First, she promised that she and her son would do nothing to hurt Elizabeth or her realm, or to encourage the alteration of religion in England. Then she offered to recognize Elizabeth as the reigning monarch, in return for Elizabeth's recognition of her son's right to the succession. Finally, she gave her word that she and her son would enter a 'perfect league' with Elizabeth as soon as the negotiations were undertaken. Greatly encouraged, Elizabeth sent another councillor, Sir Walter Mildmay, to work with Beale to negotiate a treaty, but she warned Mary 'if you shall not in the course of proceeding use that plainness and integrity that you profess, you shall greatly discourage us hereafter to yield so far forth as presently we have done'.[83]

The discussions, which began in June 1583 and continued intermittently through 1584, turned out to be Mary's last chance to obtain her freedom and restoration to the Scottish throne. Why did this attempt at settlement fail? The main reason was James VI's attitude. He had no intention of ruling alongside his mother, even if she were only a sleeping partner, and his advisers also warned him that her presence in Scotland might destabilize his rule. James, therefore, proved unhelpful from the outset. In late 1584 he further undermined the negotiations when his agents intimated that he was ready to sign an alliance with Elizabeth that would not involve his mother or demand her release. He dealt the death blow on 11 March 1585, when he sent Mary a letter saying that he did not want to enter into a treaty with her. Mary could hardly believe her

son would betray her in this way, and tried to convince herself that others were responsible for the decision: 'I am so grievously offended at the impiety and ingratitude that my child has been constrained to commit against me,' she wrote despairingly.[84] The next year, however, when she heard that James had signed a treaty with Elizabeth that made no mention of her, Mary faced the truth and blamed her son for what she saw as an act of betrayal. To be fair, though, James had no reason to be sentimental about a mother whom he could not remember and who, he was assured, had murdered his father.

La Royne d'Escosse Douairiere de france Ayant entendu comme po
obuier a tous attemptatz contre la vie de la Royne d'Anglre sa bonne soeur auroit es
nagueres faict entre aulcuns des principaulx seigneurs de ce Royaulme (vne Associatō
generalle desirant en cela comme en toutes aultres choses donner toute preuue a lad
Royne d'Angleterre sa bonne soeur de sa tresentiere affection et sincerité vers elle
et se tenant comme sa plus proche parente obligée en debuoir et sa preseruation
ha de sa bonne pure et franche volonte declare et promis suiuant lad Asso-
=siation declare et promcet en parole de Royne et sur sa foy et honneur qu'elle
repute desa present et tiendra a perpetuité pour ses mortels ennemis tous ceulx
sans nul excepter qui par Conseil procurement consentement ou aultre acte
quelconque attempteront ou executeront (ce que Dieu ne veuille) aulcune
chose au preiudice de la vie de ladite Royne sa bonne soeur et comme telx
les poursuiuera par tous moyens Jusques a l'extremité sans iamais cesser
qu'elle n'en aye faict faire Justice punition et vengeance suffizantes et
exemplares. En tesmoing dequoy et confirmation de lad Associatō
pour estre notiffie a tous ceulx quil appertiendra lad Royne d'Escosse
ha signe ce present acte desa main. A Winckfield le vme Jour
de Januier mil cinq cens quatre vingte et cinq. /

Ainsy signé   Marie R

This same J Robert Beale
seen vnder the hand and
seale of y Scottish Queen
remayning ns to Secretary
Walsingham ..

Without James's cooperation, Mary's restoration was impossible. Yet even before he had made his position clear, Mary had demonstrated that her word could not be trusted and that releasing her would consequently be unwise. Thanks to Walsingham's spy network, Elizabeth learnt in late 1583 that Mary had continued corresponding with Mendoza, who was up to his neck in conspiracy. In November of that year a Catholic gentleman, Francis Throckmorton, who had been under surveillance for several months, was arrested, and under torture he revealed details of an invasion plot involving the Guises, Pope Gregory XIII and the Jesuit leader Robert Persons. His confession implicated Mendoza directly in the plot, and disclosed Mary's correspondence with the conspirators.

Like the Ridolfi plot of 1571, the Throckmorton plot did Mary immeasurable harm. The least damaging outcome was the expulsion of Mendoza from England, which eroded Mary's opportunities for intrigue. Far more serious was the outcry amongst Elizabeth's Protestant subjects, who on hearing of the plot wanted immediate reprisals against Mary. Their case was bolstered in July 1584 by the news reaching England that a Catholic assassin had shot dead William of Orange, the Protestant leader of the rebels against Spain in the Low Countries. Elizabeth was thought to be next on the Catholic hit-list, and in order to deter an assassination attempt on her, the Privy Council drew up a document (known as the Bond of Association) that would pledge its signatories

to kill any person who might benefit from the queen's murder, whether or not the attempt was successful. The idea was that Mary would be killed summarily without any trial if anyone plotted to assassinate Elizabeth, even if Mary was ignorant of the plot or had not given it her approval. Even more unfairly, the bond also decreed that the heir of the intended beneficiary would be included within the terms of the bond. In other words, James would be executed or, more likely, excluded from the succession if any attempt were made on Elizabeth's life.

This Bond of Association was distributed throughout England to collect signatures. Although some Protestants objected to it on legal grounds, thousands of men and some women put their names to the document. Even Mary subscribed to it, but by this time her assurances of innocence in plots were thought meaningless. In late November 1584 the bond was brought before parliament to be given statutory force. Elizabeth was aghast: the proposal both smacked of lynch law and interfered with the hereditary rights of monarchs. Thanks to her intervention, the bill was modified on two important counts. First, a clause was inserted that provided for a tribunal to try and judge Mary or any other person on whose behalf the murder of Elizabeth had been attempted. Second, James was not to be barred from the succession unless it was proved that he had assented to or known about an assassination plot. In 1585 this measure was given the royal approval as an Act for the Surety of the Queen's Person.

In early 1585 Mary was in a desperate state. Her hopes for release and a new life in Scotland had been dashed; her chances of inheriting the throne of England were negligible; and her life depended upon the restraint of her friends and the mercy of Elizabeth, neither of which could be guaranteed. If the future looked bleak, the present grew more uncomfortable. In August 1584 Mary was removed from the Talbots and placed in the custody of Sir Ralph Sadler at Wingfield Manor; then, in January 1585, she was moved to the damp and gloomy castle of Tutbury, and in April given a new custodian, the brusque and utterly unsympathetic Sir Amyas Paulet. The geographical move to Tutbury was made for security reasons, but the new custodianship of the Talbots came to an end, in part because of the personal disagreements between Mary and Bess.

When Mary arrived at Tutbury she found it so barely furnished that she complained to the queen. Mary's first encounter with Paulet went badly too. His first action was to take down the cloth of estate that denoted her queenship, and he refused to listen to her tearful protests. The security at Tutbury was tighter than ever before: Mary and her servants were confined indoors; no letters from them could be dispatched; the only messages Mary was allowed to receive came through the French ambassador in London, and these were unsealed and read by Paulet; Mary's alms-giving to the poor of the region was stopped, as were her payments to servants outside her own household for fear that the money was

intended as bribes. Regular searches of her rooms and linen took place. Even with these precautions, Paulet obsessively fretted that Mary might be passed messages by laundresses who resided outside the castle, and he asked if he could initiate a body search.

Towards the end of 1585 Mary's complaints about Tutbury bore fruit, and on Christmas Eve she was removed to Chartley Hall in Staffordshire. This manor house, which belonged to the young Earl of Essex, was thought to be a secure place because it was surrounded by a deep moat. Much to Paulet's relief, the laundresses lodged within the house, leaving no possibility of Mary receiving any secret communication from the outside world: 'I cannot imagine how it may be possible for them to convey a piece of paper as big as my finger,' wrote Paulet confidently to Walsingham.[85] Walsingham, however, did intend Mary to develop contacts outside in order to spring a trap that would demonstrate her treachery to Elizabeth and provide incriminating evidence at a future trial.

On 16 January 1586 a brewer based at nearby Burton smuggled into Chartley two letters, which were wrapped in a watertight casing and hidden in the bunghole of a beer keg The first letter was written by Mary's agent in Paris, an English Catholic exile, Thomas Morgan, who introduced the writer of the second letter. He was Gilbert Gifford, an English Catholic who offered to act as a secret conductor of messages between Mary and her friends by way of the brewer. Mary was delighted,

Babington. The cyphre, wherein all passed.

a . b . c . d . e . f . g . h . i . k . l . m . n . o . p . q . r . s . t . v . x . y . z

Nulles. . Dowbletts .

and . for . with that . yf . but . wher . as . of . the . from . by . so
2 . 3 . 4 . 2 . 4l . 2 . of . when . ther . the . in . which . is . what . say . me . my . whith . sen
lre . receue . berer . I . pray you . m tee . your name . mine .

by this cyphre their lrs passed.

The newe intended Cyphre.

a . b . c . d . e . f . g . h . i . k . l . m . n . o p . q . r . s . t v . x . y . z

et	w	th	sh	ea	q		Nulles.
							Humbers. 1 . 2 . 3 . 4 . 5 . 6 . 7 . 8 . 9 .

This note ⌐ after my caracter will double the same .

this note ꝺ shall serue to annulle the precedent caracter whatsoeuer it be.

To conclude the parenthesis ss .

for punctuating at the ende of the sentence .

believing that after more than a year of total isolation she had found a safe way to communicate with her friends in England and abroad. Little did she dream that the brewer was in the pay of Walsingham and that Gifford was a double agent. She had, therefore, no idea that letters smuggled in and out of Chartley would be first forwarded to Walsingham, who would then have his master decipherer, Thomas Phelippes, decode and make copies of them, before they were replaced in the keg.

Gifford soon made contact with other Catholic exiles besides Morgan, notably the priest John Ballard and ex-soldier John Savage, who had devised a scheme to assassinate Elizabeth. In May 1586 Ballard and Savage drew into their plot Anthony Babington, a young Catholic gentleman from Derbyshire, who was persuaded to arrange for the rescue of Mary and an English rising of Catholics to be synchronized with the murder of Elizabeth. Mendoza (now based in Paris) was also enlisted by this group of Catholics; his task was to arrange for an invasion of foreign powers to be mounted from abroad.

OPPOSITE

Keys to the cipher used in Mary's correspondence with Anthony Babington. Babington wrote to Mary about a plot to rescue her and kill Elizabeth. The letters written in cipher were smuggled into Chartley in a beer keg (British Library, Additional MS 48027, f. 313v)

Unquestionably, then, a Catholic plot existed in 1586 and was not simply the fantasy of an agent provocateur, as some of Mary's apologists have suggested. However, this plot posed no actual danger to the queen or the state. Right from the start, Walsingham knew all its details and, had he wished, could have arrested all the conspirators. The secretary had in his possession the correspondence passing between Mary and her friends, while his agents were keeping a close eye on the major players in England and France. Walsingham, nevertheless, bided his time and let the plot foment. His plan was to obtain evidence against Mary that would hold up in a court of law, and he was therefore waiting until Mary's written assent to the assassination of Elizabeth and invasion of England fell into his hands.

In the summer of 1586 Walsingham's patience was rewarded. On 6 July, in response to a letter from Mary, Babington sent her full details of the plot. He told her of the plans for an invasion from abroad and the insurrection by the English Catholics, and he relayed his intentions to take ten men and 'a hundred of followers' in his charge to rescue Mary from Chartley and to send another six men 'for the dispatch of the usurper, from the obedience of whom we are by the excommunication of her made free'.[86] Mary received this communication on 14 July, and, although Nau advised her not to reply to it, she sent Babington a letter on 17 July approving his plans. Desperate to escape from the intolerable imprisonment at Chartley, and in despondency at her son's abandonment, she decided on a reckless course and committed herself openly to an enterprise against Elizabeth. Admittedly, she did not explicitly approve the queen's assassination, but she did suggest that her own escape be timed to take place before 'the six gentlemen' set to work rather than afterwards. She also did 'greatly praise and commend' the foreign enterprise against the Protestant regime in England, and promised 'to recompense' those who worked 'for my delivery'.[87] She demanded to know further details of the plot, and made a number of suggestions. Phelippes thought all this was enough to incriminate Mary. Sending the deciphered text on to Walsingham, he endorsed the copy with a small picture of the gallows on its seal. At the same time, he added to the letter sent on to Babington a forged postscript, purportedly from Mary, asking the names of the six assassins. Babington immediately smelt a rat and fled.

Babington's flight precipitated a round-up of the conspirators, and all of them were brought to London for interrogation. On 11 August 1586 an emissary from Elizabeth arrived at Chartley to announce that the Babington plot had been uncovered. Ironically, Mary was out hunting when he and his companions arrived, and seeing a group of horsemen riding towards her, she thought it was the rescue party she was expecting. Cruelly disappointed, she tried to resist when she was separated from her secretaries and ordered to accompany Elizabeth's messenger. However, she had no choice but to go with them to Tixall Hall, a few miles away. She remained there a fortnight

while her quarters at Chartley were thoroughly searched. Mary returned to find her possessions rifled; and just over a week afterwards Paulet was ordered to confiscate her money.

In September 1586 Babington, Ballard, Savage and four other English Catholics were convicted of treason and publicly executed. Meanwhile, Mary's secretaries were interrogated and admitted that they had penned her letters to Babington. At this point Mary was convinced that she would die, though whether by poison or the axe she was not yet sure. Her thoughts consequently turned to the manner of her death, and she was determined to be seen to die as a Catholic martyr. During the early 1570s she had written a long penitential poem, *Méditation,* and a short religious sonnet, both of which were included in a book edited by the Bishop of Ross and printed in Paris in 1574. These works were designed to retrieve her reputation and present her to the Catholic world as a woman of deep spirituality and true faith. Now, in 1586, Mary took every care to publicize her commitment to her faith and present herself as a victim, dying for the Catholic Church. As she wrote to the Duke of Guise in September:

OPPOSITE

Babington's confession of 21 August 1586. He confesses to communications with Mary and Mendoza to raise the country 'for the just defence of our bodies, lives and lands against the violence of the puritans'. He also repeats the standard Catholic charges against Leicester, then in the Low Countries. (British Library, Additional MS 48027, f. 306)

The Q: Lres advised that vppon returne of aunswere from Men
doza, not assuraunce that all thinge requisite, was in a readines, that
and not before it shoulde be requisite to sownde the Countrie, and to
vncover the prouission & preparation, it shoulde be geven out that what
they did was not vppon anie will for disloyall disposition towardes
the Q: but for the iust defence of or bodies, life and landes, against
the violence of the puritains &/ the principall wherof being in the Lonar,
conteyning not the these partis of the realme, purposed at his returne
to ruin not only the whole Catholiques, but also ment to depriue
her matie of her Crowne, if she did not conforme herself wholy
vnto his will, and that therefore this preparation was likewise for
the defence of her matie, and her lawfull successor: not meaninge
her send wth pretence an associatioñ might be made.

Wth beinge don and all thinge in readines both wthin and wthout
the realme, it shoulde be time for to set the fixe gent: to
worke, taking order that presently thervppon she may be taken
awaye, and because the time woulde be vncerteyne, vppon the
exploite of her great psoñ, therfore she thought it convenient
that there shoulde be some well for to gent: allwaies to attende
to bringe worde post in the Countrey, and by severall wayes, for
feare of intercepting, And further that it were good to cut of
the ordinarie poste betwixt the Court and that place.

She advised me to deale carefully and vigilantly for effectu
ing the enterprise in such sorte that it might take good effecte,
by the grace of God, affirminge that she shoulde dye contentedly,
whensoever wthstanding of or delivery out of the servitude wherin
we were holden as slaves.

Vnto wch Lre I made no aunswere, then that she shoulde vnderstande
what resolution was taken vppon her proposition, in the meane time
that I suspected one Mawde Cwho came over wth Ballard Had
discovered the plott, and indaungered vs deeply, wch how I woulde
vppon she shoulde vnderstande by the next.

                    Anthony Babington

                    Confessed subscribed and written by him self the 2j
                    of August 1586.
                         T. Bromley   W. Burleigh
                    Chrystofer Hatton. Ff. walsingham.

Sr becausse I hope yow will be here to morrow, I wryte the lesse
though / meany thyngs fall uppon me here, by ye secretaryes
Infirmytes, yet I fynd we cann so mitigeat, and vary
as to determy what shall be to be donne uppon the wryttē
report of ye stat lof ye how surveys as att your comyng
is to be seene

The Mary hath determyned forthwyyay to be ye place, for
ye scott Qu. and thir case ys be short order is gyven
for hir remove, so as she is to be at fotheryg: ye
Mich. eve at ye fardest / and our sitt assebl. at
westm̄ must be ye 27 /

and I thynk we ar to be at fotheryng ye vth of
october and I thynk yow ar lyke to be, if yow lack
not of your will at Hedelby about ye 3 or 4 /

fro wydsor castle xvj sept. 1586

Your assured lov: fr
Burghley

Trial and Execution

OPPOSITE
A letter from Lord Burghley, dated 16 September 1586, informing the recipient that Elizabeth had named Fotheringhay Castle in Northamptonshire as the place for Mary's trial. An order, he says, has been given for Mary's removal so that she shall be there by Michaelmas Eve (28 September) at the latest and 'our first assembly at Westminster' (i.e. parliament) shall open on the 27th. The lords shall all arrive at Fotheringhay, he thinks, by 5 October. (British Library, Egerton 2124, f. 36, enlarged)

BELOW
Burghley's diagram of a seating plan for the trial in the Great Chamber at Fotheringhay. The empty chair of state (top) represents the absent Queen of England, and in the centre is the chair on which Mary was supposed to sit. The two queens are divided by a table at which four justices and the

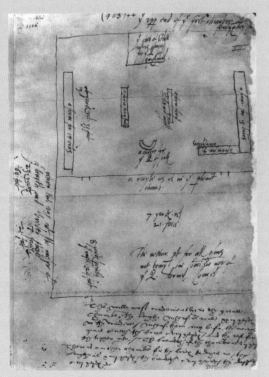

queen's council are to sit. The line shown behind Mary's seat is a rail 'as is in the parliament chamber'.
(British Library, Cotton Caligula C IX, f. 635)

ABOVE
Pencil and ink drawing of Mary's trial on 15 October 1586, preserved as part of Robert Beale's account. This tallies closely with Burghley's diagram (left), though the seat for Mary opposite the throne has been shifted to the top right-hand side to make space for members of the Privy Council. Mary is shown twice: being led in by two of her ladies, and at A. seated on the right.
(British Library, Additional MS 48027)

'For myself, I am resolute to die for my religion... With God's help, I shall die in the Catholic faith'.[88]

On 21 September 1586 Mary was led away to the place where her trial would be held, Fotheringhay Castle in Northamptonshire. Elizabeth had fussed about where to send her, rejecting the Tower of London, amongst other suggestions, before finally agreeing to Fotheringhay. In truth, Elizabeth was finding it hard to make any decision about Mary. She had been dismayed at the evidence implicating Mary in an assassination plot, and knew that her subjects would insist on the judicial death of the Scottish queen. Yet Elizabeth's instincts rebelled against putting an anointed sovereign on trial; she feared the constitutional implications, and was deeply troubled about how Mary's trial and execution would be received at foreign courts. She was also concerned about how posterity would judge her conduct. Consequently, Elizabeth prevaricated and resisted the advice of her councillors on relatively trivial matters, such as where the trial should be held and who should attend.

Mary arrived at Fotheringhay on 25 September, and her trial was fixed for mid-October. It was organized according to the terms of the 1585 Act for the Surety of the Queen's Person, which stipulated that at least twenty-four peers and privy councillors had to be appointed as commissioners to hear the case. In the event, thirty-one attended, together with five senior judges. One of the appointed commissioners was Shrewsbury, who had tried to avoid this unwelcome service by pleading sickness, but Burghley advised him that 'I see her Majesty very sorry that your Lordship should be absent at that day lest there might be of the malicious some sinister interpretation'.[89] The earl attended, though a number of the other men appointed did not turn up. All the details of the trial were planned carefully: where Mary should sit, who should attend, and the exact layout of the physical space.

The trial opened on Friday 14 October 1586 in a spacious chamber directly above the Great Hall at Fotheringhay. In the couple of days beforehand, Mary had consistently refused to acknowledge the legality of the court on the grounds that she 'was no subject'. 'I am an absolute Queen,' she pronounced, 'and will do nothing which may be prejudicial either to Royal Majesty or to other Princes of my place and rank, or my son.'[90] Recognizing the court's right of jurisdiction would injure her status and set a harmful precedent. Mary did consent, however, to appear before the commissioners in order to deny the charge that she had conspired to have Elizabeth murdered, and at nine o'clock on the first morning of the trial she limped into the hall with an escort of soldiers, accompanied by her remaining servants. She wore her usual black, with a white cambric cap on her head, to which was attached a long white veil of gauze. She steadfastly denied the charge against her, and when confronted with the copies of her correspondence to Babington and other conspirators, she demanded to see the originals, which she correctly judged they had burnt. She also put up a good fight when presented with the confessions of Babington and her two secretaries. She pointed out that their deposition could not be trusted, especially as the secretaries had not been called as witnesses against her. They had lied, she claimed, from fear of torture and death. She declared that 'I am not to be convicted but by mine own words or hand-writing' and again called upon the prosecution to produce 'the minutes of my correspondence written by myself'.[91]

Throughout the two-day proceedings, Mary's defence relied on her not having given the order for, or consent to, Elizabeth's assassination. As far as the other charges were concerned, she argued that as a queen imprisoned illegally, she had a perfect right to call on foreign powers, or disaffected Catholic subjects, to help her escape. If they chose also to overturn the government and depose the queen, that was up to them, but she had not made that decision, nor agreed to such action. Such a defence was pure casuistry, and, not surprisingly, it cut little ice with her judges. Mary's other ploy was to win the sympathy of the spectators present by emphasizing the poor state of her health and memory: 'I cannot walk without assistance nor use my arms, and I spend most of my time confined to bed by sickness.' She also tried to work on their sympathies by drawing attention to the unfairness of the trial, in that she had to answer a barrage of accusations without any preparation or representation. In her final speech to the tribunal she demanded to be

heard in 'a full parliament' or else before the queen. She then stood up 'with great presence of countenance' and regally exited the room. With nothing to lose, for a guilty verdict was inevitable, Mary had performed admirably before the court. She held up well to the hostile questioning, gave consistent responses, and for the most part retained her composure and dignity.

Elizabeth found the proceedings unbearable, and still hoped to find some other resolution to the crisis. At the last minute she sent a message to Burghley, ordering him to prorogue the court for ten days and dismiss the commissioners before any verdict could be given. During those ten days no other possibility emerged, so on 25 October the court reconvened in Star Chamber at Westminster to review the evidence against Mary and deliver its verdict. On this occasion Shrewsbury did stay away on account of his illness; perhaps he felt he had done enough to silence malicious tongues. In Star Chamber Mary's secretaries were produced, cross-examined, and made to swear on oath that their written statements were truthful. The accused queen was then found guilty and condemned to death.

Even now, Elizabeth held back from proclaiming the judicial decision and issuing the death warrant. From her behaviour and speeches, it seems that she had it in mind to offer Mary a pardon in return for her confession and request for forgiveness. Elizabeth possibly also hoped that one of her subjects would remember his oath in the Bond of Association and take the law into his own hands. Her privy councillors, however, were determined on a public execution, and in order to force their queen to be resolute, they applied pressure through the parliament that had been summoned to discuss the issue. The Commons and Lords presented the queen with a joint petition urging the immediate execution of Mary. Elizabeth promised to think about it, but twelve days later, on 24 November 1586, she asked parliament whether it could not find some other way to deal with Mary that would not put her own life at risk. Parliament gave a firm 'no'. 'I have just cause to complain,' replied Elizabeth, 'that I, who have in my time pardoned so many rebels, winked at so many treasons...should now be forced to this proceeding against such a person.' What would her enemies say, she continued, when they learnt that 'for the safety of herself, a maiden queen could be content to spill the blood, even of her own kinswoman'? She asked them, therefore, to be content with 'an answer answerless'.[92] The pressure on Elizabeth, however, proved too much, and on 4 December she issued a proclamation declaring Mary's guilt and the sentence of death. At the same time, a pamphlet containing edited versions of her November speeches to parliament appeared in booksellers' shops. Elizabeth wanted her deep reluctance to execute a queen to be widely known.

At the same time as Elizabeth was experiencing this domestic pressure to order Mary's execution, foreign ambassadors were urging her to hold back. Henri III of France sent a special envoy to raise points of law concerning the case, while the resident French ambassador tried to intercede on Mary's behalf. Several envoys also arrived from James VI on missions to save Mary, and in January 1587 James wrote Elizabeth a personal letter imploring her to grant his 'so long continued and so earnest request' to spare the life of his mother.[93] As Elizabeth was inclined to waver in the face of this diplomatic activity, Burghley and Walsingham took action. To silence the French, Walsingham produced spurious evidence of their ambassador's involvement in a plot against Elizabeth. To counteract the influence of James, rumours were spread that the Scottish king could be bought off with assurances about the succession. Yet Elizabeth still did not sign the death warrant.

In contrast to Elizabeth, Mary was calmly awaiting her death. According to one near-contemporary account, on the publication of the death sentence 'so far was she from being

OPPOSITE

Drawing of Mary's execution, 8 February 1587 by Robert Beale. Mary is shown three times: she enters at the top left preceded by Thomas Andrews, the sheriff of the county (numbered 5); facing the onlookers (centre), she is disrobed by her attendants, Jane Kennedy and Elizabeth Curle; finally, she appears on the block (top right on platform). The Earls of Shrewsbury and Kent are seated to the left (1 and 2), and the Dean of Peterborough stands below (6). In a row at the back of the hall (7) stand the four men of her household who were allowed to attend her: Robert Melville, 'her poticary [sic], surgeon and one other old man besides'. The scaffold was draped in black. (British Library, Additional MS 48027, f. 650*)

dismayed thereat that with a settled and steadfast countenance, lifting up her eyes and hands towards heaven, she gave thanks to God for it'.[94] Over the next weeks she made 'no mention of desire of life', and 'with many shows of constancy' she displayed no fear of death.[95] Much to Paulet's annoyance, she refused to admit her 'odious' crimes, as Elizabeth demanded, but continued to maintain that she was the innocent victim of all those in England who hated the Catholic Church. In her farewell letters to friends, family and foreign rulers, she upheld this position and declared her readiness to die for the Catholic faith. When writing to Pope Sixtus, she begged him to permit the King of Spain to take on her rights to the English crown if her son did not convert to Catholicism.

With no word about the execution for weeks on end, Mary's nerves began to fray, but at last, on 1 February 1587, Elizabeth signed the death warrant. News of a further plot and rumours of a foreign invasion seem to have forced her hand. As Walsingham was ill, she handed the warrant over to her junior secretary, William Davison, and told him to keep it secret from everyone except Walsingham. But she was still uneasy. Hoping to offload the responsibility, she ordered Davison to send Paulet a letter, hinting that he should carry out the pledge made in the Bond of Association and murder his charge quietly. Paulet was appalled and refused. By this action it was evident that Elizabeth was still trying to avoid an execution, and preferred the warrant not to be used. Her

privy councillors, however, had had enough of the queen's nervousness and vacillations. Burghley called ten councillors to a secret meeting in his private chambers and arranged for the warrant to be dispatched.

Beale took it to Fotheringhay. Accompanying him to the castle were Shrewsbury and the Earl of Kent, who were charged to carry out the commission. Arriving on Tuesday 7 February, Beale read out the warrant and told Mary that she would be executed the following morning. Mary received the news calmly: 'I thank you for such welcome news. You will do me a great good in withdrawing me from this world out of which I am very glad to go.' In her new-found role as a Catholic martyr, she expressed her joy at shedding her blood for her God and 'the Catholic Church, and to maintain its right in this country'. She swore her innocence to all charges against her on the Bible. When Kent objected that it was a Catholic Bible, she retorted: 'if I swear on the book which I believe to be the true version, will not your lordship believe my oath more than if I were to swear on a translation in which I do not believe?'[96] Mary then made a number of requests, including the presence of her Catholic chaplain to give her communion and confession, all of which were refused. The rest of the evening she spent with her servants, eating a small meal and drinking with them a cup of wine before kneeling in prayer. Returning to business, she made her will, distributed her possessions, and, after midnight, sat down to write her very last letter. The recipient was Henri III, and the text was clearly intended for circulation as she penned it in her best handwriting. In it she claimed that the two causes of her execution were her Catholic faith and her God-given right to the English throne. She also asked the king to look after her faithful servants and to offer prayers 'for a queen who has herself been called Most Christian and who dies a Catholic stripped of all her possessions'.[97]

The following morning Mary was escorted to the Great Hall by Shrewsbury and Kent. Knowing that the execution would not only be in public, but also reported afterwards, she took care again to portray herself as a Catholic martyr. Holding a crucifix in one hand and a Latin prayer book in the other, with a rosary attached to her girdle and an *Agnus Dei* (a medallion bearing an image of Christ as the Lamb of God) around her neck, she went to her death flaunting the symbols of Roman Catholicism. She was also dressed in the colours of a Catholic martyr: under an outer gown of thick black satin trimmed with gold embroidery and sable, she wore a bodice of dark blood-coloured crimson and a petticoat of the same colour. The words she spoke were designed to convey the same effect: 'Be the bearer of this news,' she ordered her steward on her way to the hall, 'that I die a Catholic, firm in my religion, a faithful Scotch woman and a true French woman. God forgive those who have sought my death.'[98]

Mary entered the hall with her servants. Gathered there were perhaps some three hundred spectators as she made her way to the scaffold in the centre.[99] On her face was a cheerful and carefree smile, and she remained silent until Dr Richard Fletcher, the Dean of Peterborough Cathedral, stepped forward to deliver a Protestant sermon. 'Mr Dean,' she chided him, 'I am settled in the ancient Catholic Roman religion, and mind to spend my blood in defence of it.' She refused to join in the prayers for the same reason, and read aloud from her Latin prayer book instead, trying with her servants to drown out the Protestant voices in prayer. When the prayers had finished, she switched to English and called on God to avert his wrath from England, and invoked the saints to intercede for her soul. Ignoring a protest from Kent, she eventually ended her prayers, kissing the crucifix and making the sign of the cross, liturgical acts offensive to most committed Protestants. Then her women took off Mary's black gown to reveal her wearing the liturgical colour of martyrdom in the Catholic Church. She covered her arms with sleeves of the same colour, and her white veil was removed. A white *Corpus Christi* cloth embroidered with gold was wrapped over her eyes, and the ends were pinned to make a turban on her head. She knelt on the cushion before the block, recited a Latin psalm, and then put her head on the block, stretching out her arms. 'In your hands, O Lord, I commend my spirit,' she cried out in Latin. But then events went less smoothly. The executioner's first blow missed the neck full on, only cutting it with a glancing blow and causing her to utter an involuntary noise. It took a second strike to sever her neck, except for one small sinew, which had to be

sawed away. When her head was lifted aloft, Mary's lips were still moving, and her auburn wig fell to the ground.

Mary's body was immediately embalmed and remained at Fotheringhay for several months. At last, during the night of 30 July 1587, it was taken to Peterborough Cathedral, where a funeral service was held the following day. Her tomb was placed in the south aisle, opposite that of Queen Katherine of Aragon. There it remained until 1612, when her son, who had succeeded Elizabeth as James I, ordered her exhumation and reburial in Westminster Abbey. She was placed in the south aisle of the Lady Chapel or Henry VII Chapel, along with Margaret Beaufort, the mother of Henry VII, and Margaret Douglas, Mary's mother-in-law

and James's own paternal grandmother. Like her grandson, Charles I, Mary had a good death. Furthermore, like his, her death was fully exploited by supporters who, in pursuit of their own political gains, sought to present the executed monarch as a martyr. In Mary's case, immediately after the execution, exiled English Catholics produced memorials and verses representing her as a martyr of the Roman Church, and depicting Elizabeth as an English Jezebel (the archetypal wicked and idolatrous ruler reviled in the Old Testament). The Jesuit Robert Southwell's verse summed up the Catholic perspective:

> Alive a Queen, now dead I am a Saint
> Once Mary called, my name now
> Martyr is.[100]

But the most famous examples of the genre were Adam Blackwood's *Martyre de la Royne d'Escosse* (The History and Martyrdom of the Queen of Scotland, 1589), which provided a detailed life of the queen, including a description of her harsh treatment in England, and *La Mort de la Royne d'Escosse Douairière de France* (The Death of the Queen of Scotland and Dowager Queen of France, 1589), a fuller narrative of her death. Although Elizabeth's government mounted its own propaganda campaign, issuing pamphlets justifying her death and printing correspondence from the Babington plot, over time the pro-Marian version seems to have won the battle for the Scottish queen's reputation.

Most biographers and historians have treated Mary as a tragic figure whose fate was undeserved. Some see her as the victim of circumstance, others of a vindictive Elizabeth, and still others point to Cecil and Walsingham as the villains of the piece. However, in my view, Mary's own character brought about her undoing. While she had strengths as a ruler, including great courage and charisma, she also had serious weaknesses that affected her political judgement at crucial moments. Too often she displayed inflexibility in negotiation, proved a poor judge of character and acted too hastily under pressure. These traits helped bring about her deposition in Scotland and long captivity in England. She made enemies of Elizabeth and Cecil by insisting on her rights to the succession and refusing to ratify the Treaty of Edinburgh. She alienated the Scottish nobility by her reliance on Rizzio and her poor choice of husbands. Her ill-judged decision to leave Scotland left her supporters leaderless in the civil war that followed. The same weaknesses also did her no favours during her years in England. Her consistent refusal to make any compromises convinced Cecil, and ultimately Elizabeth, that she was an enemy of the state and unsafe to set free. Her choice of counsellors and co-conspirators when in England was most unwise, while her reckless decision to send a letter to Babington proved fatal. Whether or not Mary was an adulteress or accomplice to murder will never be satisfactorily proved, but in many ways it is irrelevant. Throughout her life, and at the end of her forty-four years, it was her flawed political judgement that caused her deposition and eventually destroyed her.

Notes

Abbreviations

CSPF   *Calendar of State Papers, Foreign:*
           Elizabeth

CSPSc   *Calendar of State Papers, Scotland*

CSPSp   *Calendar of State Papers, Spain*

CSPV   *Calendar of State Papers, Venetian*

HMC Bath   *Historical Manuscripts Commission,*
           58 Bath

In all other cases, sources are cited in full on the
first mention, and abbreviated thereafter.

1   Ralph Sadler to Henry VIII on 23 March 1543,
in Arthur Clifford (ed.), *The State Papers and
Letters of Sir Ralph Sadler*, vol. 1, p. 87
(Edinburgh, 1809).

2   Ralph Sadler to Henry VIII on 10 August
1543, ibid., p. 253.

3   The Privy Council to Edward Seymour, Earl
of Hertford, on 10 April 1544, in Joseph Bain
(ed.), *The Hamilton Papers*, vol. 2, pp. 325–6
(Edinburgh, 1892).

4   Letter of 18 August 1548, in Jane T. Stoddart,
The Girlhood of Mary Queen of Scots, pp. 411–12
(London, 1908).

5   Letter of 1 October 1548, ibid., p. 14.

6   Brézé's letter of 11 December 1548, ibid.,
pp. 425–6, and M de Lorges' letter of
19 December 1548, in Margaret Wood (ed.),
*Foreign Correspondence with Marie de Lorraine
1548–57*, Scottish History Society, Third
Series, vol. 7, p. 21 (Edinburgh, 1925).

7   Stoddart, *Girlhood of Mary*, p. 41.

8   Anne de Montmorency to Marie on
24 December 1551, in Wood (ed.), *Foreign
Correspondence*, vol. 7, p. 104.

9   Anne d'Este to Marie in 1552, ibid., p. 110.

10   25 February 1553, in Stoddart, *Girlhood of
Mary*, p. 101.

11   The Cardinal of Guise's letter to Marie on
18 August 1556, in John H. Pollen, *Papal
Negotiations with Mary Queen of Scots
1561–1567*, Scottish History Society, First
Series, pp. 420–1 (Edinburgh, 1901).

12   25 April 1558, *CSPV, 1557–8*, p. 1486.

13   Mary's letter to her mother dated 24 April
1558, in D. Hay Fleming, *Mary Queen of Scots
from Her Birth to Her Flight in England*, p. 492
(London, 1897).

14   9 November 1557, *CSPV, 1557–8*, p. 1365.

15   Report of 30 May 1559, in Patrick Forbes,
*A Full View of Public Transactions in the Reign
of Queen Elizabeth*, vol. 1, p. 113 (London,
1741).

16   Sir Nicholas Throckmorton to Cecil on
21 June 1559, ibid., p. 136.

17   *CSPF, 1558–9*, p. 314.

18   Sir John Mason's letter of 18 March 1559 and
Throckmorton's letter of 24 May 1559, in
CSPF, 1558–9, pp. 179 and 272–3.

19   Throckmorton's reports of 11 and 13 July 1559,
in Forbes, *Full View*, vol. 1, p. 157.

20   Throckmorton's reports of 25 August 1559,
and a letter from two English envoys on
14 November 1559, ibid., pp. 210 and 261.

21   Throckmorton's report of 28 April 1560,
National Archives, SP70/13, f. 229.

22 30 June 1560, *CSPV, 1558–80*, p. 234.

23 Throckmorton's letter to Elizabeth dated 17 November 1560, in Philip Yorke, 2nd Earl of Hardwicke (ed.), *Miscellaneous State Papers, 1501–1726*, vol. 1, p. 131.

24 Throckmorton's report of 31 December 1560, in Robert S. Rait, *Mary Queen of Scots: Scottish History from Contemporary Writers*, p. 11 (Second Edition, London, 1900).

25 Throckmorton's report of 23 June 1561, National Archives, SP70/27, f. 56.

26 This quotation comes from the *Discours de la Reine d'Escosse Jadis Reine de France par le Sieur de Brantôme*, printed in *Mémoires de Michel de Castelnau*, vol. 1, p. 536 (Brussels, 1731). Although it cannot be entirely trusted, it appears in many secondary sources, most recently in John Guy, *My Heart Is My Own: The Life of Mary Queen of Scots*, p. 133 (London, 2004).

27 *John Knox's History of the Reformation*, ed. and trans. by William Croft Dickinson, vol. 1, p. 8 (London, 1949).

28 Ibid., vol. 2, p. 17.

29 Throckmorton's report of 23 June 1561, National Archives, SP70/ 27, f. 56v.

30 Mortimer Levine, *Tudor Dynastic Problems, 1460–1571*, pp. 177–8 (Letchworth, 1973).

31 5 January 1561, Alexandre Labanoff (ed.), *Lettres et Mémoires de Marie, Reine d'Ecosse*, vol. 1, p. 127 (London, 1844).

32 Cecil's memorandum of 20 June 1562, British Library, Cotton Caligula B IX, ff. 209–12.

33 Letter Patent of 24 August 1562, Labanoff, *Lettres*, vol. 1, p. 154.

34 Sir Henry Sidney's letter to Cecil dated 25 July 1562, *CSPSc, 1547–63*, p. 641.

35 Thomas Randolph's letter to Cecil dated 18 September 1562, ibid., p. 651.

36 *Knox's History*, vol. 2, p. 82.

37 Randolph's report of 5 March 1564, British Library, Cotton Caligula B X, f. 265.

38 15 August 1562, *The Register of the Privy Council of Scotland, 1545–69*, p. 217 (Edinburgh, 1877).

39 Randolph's letters of 1 April and 13 and 21 December 1563, *CSPSc, 1563–9*, pp. 2 and 29.

40 Gordon Donaldson (ed.), *The Memoirs of Sir James Melville of Halhill*, p. 45 (London, 1969).

41 Randolph's letter to Cecil dated 17 March 1565, *CSPSc, 1563–9*, p. 136.

42 Randolph's letter to Cecil dated 8 May 1563, ibid., p. 156.

43 Randolph's letter to Cecil dated 3 June 1565, ibid., p. 173.

44 Victor Von Klarwill, *Queen Elizabeth and Some Foreigners*, p. 251 (London, 1928).

45 Report of Captain Cockburn, 2 October 1565, National Archives, SP52/ 11, f. 116v.

46 Randolph's letters in Robert Keith (ed.), *History of the Affairs of Church and State in Scotland*, vol. 2, p. 268 (Edinburgh, 1845).

47 Mary's letter of 2 April 1566, ibid., p. 419.

48 Donaldson, *Melville's Memoirs*, p. 56.

49 Ibid., p. 57.

50 The Earl of Bedford's report, in Hay Fleming, *Mary Queen of Scots*, p. 136.

51 Monsieur Le Croc's report of 15 October 1566, in Keith, *History*, vol. 2, p. 451.

52 Buchanan's *Ane Detectioun*, in James Anderson, *Collections Relating to Mary Queen of Scots*, vol. 2, p. 10 (Edinburgh, 1727).

53 24 October 1566, in Keith, *History*, vol. 2, p. 467 note.

54 Letter from Monsieur Le Croc dated 2 December 1566, ibid., p. 474, and vol. 3, Appx no. 14.

55 'Protestation of the earls of Huntly and Argyll', ibid., vol. 2, p. 475, and vol. 3, Appx no. 16.

56 Elizabeth's instructions to Bedford dated 7 November 1566, ibid., vol. 2, p. 482.

57 Letter from Henry Darnley to his father dated 7 February 1566, in Reginald Henry Mahon, *The Tragedy of Kirk o' Field*, p. 115 (Cambridge, 1930).

58 Keith, *History*, vol. 2, p. 558.

59 3 May 1567, *CVSPSp, 1558–67*, p. 638.

60 Donaldson, *Melville's Memoirs*, p. 64.

61 Ibid., p. 68.

62 Sir William Drury's letter to Cecil dated 12 June 1567, National Archives, SP 59/13, f. 146v.

63 Sir William Drury's letter to Cecil dated 18 June 1567, ibid., f. 157.

64 Ibid.

65 Hay Fleming, *Mary Queen of Scots*, p. 165.

66 1 May 1568, Labanoff, *Lettres*, vol. 2, p. 69.

67 Elizabeth's letter to Throckmorton dated 27 July 1567, Keith, *History*, vol. 2, p. 704.

68 Sir Francis Knollys' letters of 16 July 1568, in Thomas Wright (ed.), *Queen Elizabeth and Her Times*, vol. 1, p. 289 (London, 1838); and of 29 July 1568 in *Papers Relating to Mary Queen of Scots, Manuscripts from Sir William Knollys*, p. 15 (London, 1875).

69 Earl of Sussex's letter of 22 October 1568, in E. Lodge, *Illustrations of British History*, vol. 1, p. 462 (London, 1838).

70 26 December 1568, *CSPSc, 1563–9*, pp. 589–90.

71 Cecil answer of 10 January 1569, in Gordon Donaldson, *The First Trial of Mary Queen of Scots*, p. 154 (London, 1969).

72 Elizabeth's letter of 7 November 1568, in *Knollys' Papers*, p. 55.

73 John Daniel Leader, *Mary Queen of Scots in Captivity*, pp. 23–4 (Sheffield, 1880).

74 Ibid., p. 46.

75 William Murdin, *A Collection of State Papers Relating to Affairs in the Reign of Queen Elizabeth from the Year 1571 to 1596*, p. 180 (London, 1759).

76 Antonia Fraser, *Mary Queen of Scots*, p. 463 (London, 1969).

77 British Library, Additional MS 48023, f. 147v.

78 Arguments against Mary presented to Elizabeth by some of both Houses of Parliament, 26 May [1572], in T. Hartley (ed.), *Proceedings in the Parliaments of Elizabeth I*, vol. 1, pp. 274–89 (Leicester, 1981).

79 Gilbert Talbot's letter of 11 May 1573, in Lodge, *Illustrations*, vol. 2, p. 19. (Gilbert was the son of George Talbot, the Earl of Shrewsbury.)

80 Shrewsbury's letter to Burghley [1580], ibid., p. 192.

81 Shrewsbury's undated letter, ibid., vol. 2, p. 192.

82 Burghley's letter of 1582, *HMC, Bath*, V, p. 40.

83 British Library, Additional MS 48049, f. 199.

84 Postscript of Mary's letter to Monsieur de Mauvissière, 12 March 1585, in Labanoff, *Lettres*, vol. 6, p. 125.

85 10 January 1586, in John Morris (ed.) *Letterbooks of Sir Amias Poulet*, p. 126 (London, 1874).

86 John H. Pollen (ed.), *Mary Queen of Scots and the Babington Plot*, Scottish History Society, Third Series, pp. 20–2 (Edinburgh, 1922).

87 Ibid., pp. 38–45.

88 Labanoff, *Lettres*, vol. 6, p. 439.

89 Burghley's letter to Shrewsbury dated 22 October 1586, *HMC Bath*, V, p. 75.

90 *William Camden's History of the Most Renowned and Victorious Princess Elizabeth*, ed. by Wallace T. MacCaffrey p. 242 (Chicago, 1970). See also Mary's third answer, *CSPSc, 1586–8*, p. 99.

91 Quotations within the narrative of the trial are taken from Francis Steuart, *Trial of Mary Queen of Scots*, pp. 38–54 (Edinburgh and London, 1922), Mrs Maxwell Scot, *The*

Tragedy of Fotheringay..., pp. 53–67 (London, 1895), *Camden's History*, pp. 247–58, and *Hardwicke State Papers*, vol. 1, pp. 224–50.

92 Hartley, *Proceedings*, vol. 2, p. 267.

93 James VI's letter to Elizabeth dated 26 January 1587, in Leah S. Marcus, Janel Mueller and Mary Beth Rose (eds), *Elizabeth I: Collected Works*, p. 282 (Chicago, 2000).

94 *Camden's History*, p. 267.

95 Paulet's letters, in Morris, *Letter-books of Paulet*, pp. 326–7 and 331.

96 Maxwell Scot, *Fotheringay*, pp. 181 and 183.

97 Labanoff, *Lettres*, vol. 6, pp. 492–3.

98 Maxwell Scot, *Fotheringay*, p. 207.

99 A description of the execution can be found in Henry Ellis, *Original Letters Illustrative of British History*, Second Series, vol. 3 (London, 1827), pp. 112–18. See also British Library Additional MS 48027, ff. 654–8v.

100 Lambeth Palace, MS 655, f. 112.

Linlithgow Palace in West Lothian. This was the birthplace of Mary, but she was removed to Stirling Castle when she was seven months old. The palace was extensively rebuilt by her grandfather, James IV, and her father, James V. (British Library, 189.g.9)

Further Reading

General

Apart from the manuscripts in the British Library, there is a wealth of material in the National Archives at Kew and the National Library of Scotland. Useful summaries of the manuscripts in England can be found in the *Calendar of the State Papers Relating to Scotland and Mary, Queen of Scots 1547–1603*, edited by Joseph Bain and others (Edinburgh, 1898–1969), the *Calendar of State Papers, Foreign: Elizabeth*, edited by J. Stevenson and others (London, 1863–1950), and the *Calendar of State Papers Relating to the Affairs of the Borders of England and Scotland*, edited by Joseph Bain (London, 1894–6). Mary's own letters and writings have been edited in seven volumes by Prince Alexandre Labanoff and entitled *Lettres et Mémoires de Marie, Reine d'Ecosse* (London, 1844). Primary material is printed in J. Anderson (ed.), *Collections Relating to Mary Queen of Scots*, 4 vols (Edinburgh, 1727–8), and Robert S. Rait has edited a useful compendium of extracts from English, Spanish and Venetian papers, as well as a variety of contemporary writers (London, 1899).

For background reading on Scottish government and politics, Julian Goodare's *State and Society in Early Modern Scotland* (Oxford, 1999) and *The Government of Scotland 1560–1625* (Oxford, 2004) are thought-provoking and helpful.

Excellent introductions to the Scottish Reformation are Gordon Donaldson's *The Scottish Reformation* (Cambridge, 1964) and I.B. Cowan's *The Scottish Reformation* (London, 1982). The religious history, however, is best traced through Robert Keith (ed.), *History of the Affairs of Church and State in Scotland, from the Beginning of the Reformation to the Retreat of Queen Mary into England, 1568*, reprinted by the Spottiswoode Society (Edinburgh, 1844–50).

Three modern biographies of Mary can be strongly recommended. The oldest, by Antonia Fraser (*Mary Queen of Scots*, London, 1969), is detailed and readable, if a little sentimental for most modern tastes. Jenny Wormald's *Mary Queen of Scots: A Study in Failure* (London, 1988) provides an astringent contrast but is perhaps too critical of the queen. The most recent biography, John Guy's *My Heart Is My Own: The Life of Mary Queen of Scots* (London, 2004) provides a revisionist account and sees William Cecil as the agent of Mary's misfortunes. All three works are scholarly and lively to read, but only Fraser writes in full about Mary's life after her flight to England.

Some earlier studies of Mary are still invaluable, notably David Hay Fleming's *Mary Queen of Scots from Her Birth to Her Flight into England* (London, 1897), which contains primary material, as well as detailed notes.

Important biographies of people who were important in Mary's life include: Pamela E. Ritchie, *Mary of Guise in Scotland 1548–1560: A Political Career* (Edinburgh, 2002), and

Maurice Lee Jr, *James Stewart, Earl of Moray: A Political Study of the Reformation in Scotland* (Westport, Conn., 1971). Caroline Bingham provides a lively account of Henry Stewart in *Darnley: A Life of Henry Stuart, Lord Darnley, Consort of Mary Queen of Scots* (London, 1997). The best biography of Bothwell is Humphrey Drummond, *The Queen's Man: James Hepburn, Earl of Bothwell and Duke of Orkney, 1536–1578* (London, 1975).

Important essays on Mary can be found in Michael Lynch (ed.), *Mary Stewart: Queen in Three Kingdoms* (Oxford, 1988).

Introduction

Ian B. Cowan, *The Enigma of Mary Stuart* (London, 1971), contains extracts from different historians illustrating the widely conflicting interpretations of Mary's character and actions. George Buchanan's history of the reign, *The Tyrannous Reign of Mary Stewart*, has been edited by W.A. Gatherer (Edinburgh, 1958), and *John Knox's History of the Reformation in Scotland* is edited and translated by W.C. Dickinson, 2 vols (London and Edinburgh, 1949).

James Emerson Phillips, in *Images of a Queen: Mary Stuart in Sixteenth Century Literature* (Berkeley, California, 1964), traces the origins of some of these interpretations. Maurice Lee, 'The Daughter of Debate: Mary, Queen of Scots, After 400 Years', *Scottish Historical Review* 68 (1989), pp. 70–80 provides a review of ten publications produced in the quarter-centenary year of her death. Jayne Elizabeth Lewis, *Mary Queen of Scots: Romance and Nation* (London, 1998), examines Mary's representation over time in musical, visual and literary works, but needs to be read critically.

CHAPTER 1
Early Life in Scotland and France 1542–1558

Marie de Guise's correspondence throws considerable light on her daughter's life in France, and is edited by Marguerite Wood for the Scottish History Society, Third Series, vols 4 and 7 (Edinburgh, 1923 and 1925). Useful printed primary material on Anglo-Scottish relations is contained in *The State Papers and Letters of Sir Ralph Sadler*, edited by Arthur Clifford (Edinburgh, 1809), and *The Letters and Papers, Foreign and Domestic, of the Reign of Henry VIII*, edited in 21 volumes by J.S. Brewer et al. (London, 1862–1932). Robin Bell has translated and edited Mary's poems in *Bittersweet within My Heart: The Love Poems of Mary Queen of Scots* (London, 1992).

For the Scottish politics of James V's reign and Mary's minority, see Jamie Cameron, *James V: The Personal Rule, 1528–1542* (East Linton, 1998), and David Byrd Franklin, *The Scottish Regency of the Earl of Arran: A Study in the Failure of Anglo-Scottish Relations* (Lampeter, 1995). Anglo-Scottish relations can best be approached through Marcus Merriman, *The Rough Wooings: Mary Queen of Scots 1542–1551* (East Linton, 2000).

Guise interests in Scotland are well explained in Stuart Carroll, *Noble Power during the French Wars of Religion: The Guise Affinity and the Catholic Cause in Normandy* (Cambridge, 1998). French policy can also be explored through Elizabeth Bonner, *The French Reactions to the Rough Wooings of Mary Queen of Scots* (Sydney, 1998).

Information about Mary's jewels and clothing can be gleaned from Joseph Robertson (ed.), *Inventaire de la Royne d'Escosse, Douairie de France, 1556–1569*, Bannatyne Club, vol. III (Edinburgh, 1863). Her education, appearance and life in France are described in Jane A. Stoddart, *The Girlhood of Mary Queen of Scots* (London, 1908). For more details on the four Maries, see T.D. Duncan, 'The Queen's Maries', *Scottish Historical Review* 2 (1905), pp. 363–71. For discussions of Mary's poems, see Lisa Hopkins, *Writing Renaissance Queens: Texts by and about Elizabeth I and Mary Queen of Scots* (Newark, Delaware, 2002), and Peter C. Herman (ed.), *Reading Monarchs' Writing: The Poetry of Henry VIII, Mary Stuart, Elizabeth I, and James VI/I* (Newark, Delaware, 2002).

CHAPTER 2

Queen-Dauphine and Queen of France 1558–1560

Mary's demeanour and behaviour during this phase of her life were closely observed by Throckmorton and other ambassadors, and can be accessed through the *Calendars of State Papers* and Patrick Forbes, *A Full View of Public Transactions in the Reign of Queen Elizabeth*, 2 vols (London, 1741).

The rebellion by the Lords of the Congregation is discussed by Ritchie (*Mary of Guise*) and Robert Keith (*History*). For Guise foreign policy and the French in Scotland see Stuart Carroll, *Guise Affair*, and for England's policy towards Scotland, see Jane E.A. Dawson, 'William Cecil and the British Dimension of Early Elizabethan Foreign Policy', *History* 74 (1989), pp. 196–216, and Stephen Alford, *The Early Elizabeth Polity: William Cecil and the British Succession Crisis, 1558–1569* (Cambridge, 1998).

CHAPTER 3

Widowed Queen of Scotland 1561–1564

In addition to the printed primary sources cited earlier, material can be found in Joseph Stevenson, *Selections from Unpublished Manuscripts in the College of Arms and the British*

Museum Illustrating the Reign of Mary Queen of Scots, Maitland Club 41 (Glasgow, 1837). For Maitland's mission, see James Hungerford Pollen, *A Letter from Mary Queen of Scots to the Duke of Guise January 1562*, First Series, vol. 43 (Edinburgh, 1904), especially pp. 37–45.

Historians do not agree about the nature or wisdom of Mary's religious policy. One sympathetic voice is Gordon Donaldson in his short biography, *Mary, Queen of Scots* (London, 1974). Another is Julian Goodare, 'The First Parliament of Mary, Queen of Scots', *Sixteenth Century Journal* 36 (2005), pp. 55–75, where he argues that Mary showed political astuteness in winning Protestant acquiescence for her regime, avoiding the ratification of Protestant legislation and sowing dissension amongst the Scottish Protestants.

For the progress through Edinburgh and the capital's relations with Mary, Michael Lynch, *Edinburgh and the Reformation* (Edinburgh, 1981) is indispensable.

For the politics and personalities in Scotland there are a number of important academic studies: Gordon Donaldson, *Scotland: James V to James VII* (Edinburgh, 1965) and *All the Queen's Men: Power and Politics in Mary Stewart's Scotland* (London, 1983); Jane E.A. Dawson, *The Politics of Religion in the Age of Mary, Queen of Scots: The Earl of Argyll and the Struggle for Britain and Ireland* (Cambridge, 2002). An entertaining read is Harry Potter, *Bloodfeud: The Stewarts and Gordons at War in the Age of Mary Queen of Scots* (Stroud, 2002).

Mary's attempt to be recognized as Elizabeth's successor is discussed in Mortimer Levine, *Tudor Dynastic Problems* (London, 1973). On Darnley's return to Scotland, see Simon Adams's essay in

Michael Lynch's collection. For Anglo-Scottish relations and the Darnley marriage, see Jane E.A. Dawson, 'Mary Queen of Scots, Lord Darnley and Anglo-Scottish Relations in 1565', *International History Review* 8 (1986), pp. 1–24.

CHAPTER 4
Married Queen of Scotland 1565–1567

Sir James Melville's *Memoirs*, which are referred to in the text, were edited originally by T. Thomson for the Bannatyne Club, vol. 18 (Edinburgh, 1827), and then by Gordon Donaldson in 1969.

Dawson, *Politics of Religion* (1986 and 2002) and Donaldson, *All the Queen's Men* (1983) are equally relevant to this chapter. The most recent analysis of Mary's involvement in Darnley's murder is A.E. MacRobert, *Mary Queen of Scots and the Casket Letters* (London and New York, 2002), which also provides in its appendices a modern and accessible copy of the full set of Casket Letters. Earlier accounts are: R.H. Mahon, *Mary Queen of Scots: A Study of the Lennox Narrative* (Cambridge, 1924) and *The Tragedy of Kirk o' Field* (Cambridge, 1930), and M.H. Armstrong Davison, *The Casket Letters: A Solution to the Mystery of Mary Queen of Scots and the Murder of Lord Darnley* (London, 1965). All discuss the evidence, but exonerate Mary. For a different conclusion see Hans Villius, 'The Casket Letters: A Famous Case Reopened', *Historical Journal* 28 (1985), pp. 517–34. He argues that the Long Glasgow letter is genuine, but was insufficiently specific to condemn Mary, so her enemies gilded the lily by adding forgeries.

Further details on the baptism of Prince James can be found in Michael Lynch, 'Queen Mary's Triumph: The Baptismal Celebrations at Stirling in December 1566', *Scottish Historical Review* 69 (1990), pp. 1–21.

CHAPTER 5
Early Years in England 1568–1572

Some of Sir Francis Knollys's letters were printed in Patrick Collinson's *The English Captivity of Mary Queen of Scots* (Sheffield, 1987). Other correspondence of Knollys's was edited anonymously for the Philobiblon Society, *Papers Relating to Mary Queen of Scots* (London, 1875).

Gordon Donaldson, *The First Trial of Mary Queen of Scots* (London, 1959) is essential reading for the tribunal held at York and London, and its wider context. For English policy and Norfolk's matrimonial scheme, see Alford's *Early Elizabethan Polity*.

CHAPTER 6
Captivity, Conspiracies and Execution 1572–1587

Much of the correspondence concerning Shrewsbury's custodianship of Mary is printed in E. Lodge, *Illustrations of British History*, vols 1 and 2 (London, 1838). Other letters that are at Longleat are calendared in *Historical Manuscripts Commission, 58 Bath*, V, pp. 20–66 *passim*. Mary's accounts at Tutbury are printed in Allan J. Crosby and John Bruce, 'Accounts and Papers Relating to Mary Queen of Scots', *Camden Society*, 93 (1867). Some papers related to the 1583–4 negotiations with Mary, her involvement in plots and her trial can be found in Conyers Read (ed.) 'The Bardon Papers: Documents Relating to the Imprisonment and Trial of Mary Queen of Scots', *Camden Society*, Third Series, 17 (1909). For the Babington Plot, the printed sources in John Hungerford Pollen, *Mary Queen of Scots and the Babington Plot* (Edinburgh, 1922) are essential. Contemporary descriptions of Mary's trial and execution are printed in A. Francis Steuart, *The Trial of Mary Queen of Scots* (Edinburgh and London, 1922) and Mrs Maxwell Scot, *The Tragedy of Fotheringay Founded on the Journal of*

D. Bourgoing, Physician to Mary Queen of Scots (London, 1895). Jayne Elizabeth Lewis, *The Trial of Mary Queen of Scots: A Brief History with Documents* (Basingstoke, 1999), includes the text of nine documents related to the trial and execution. Parliamentary speeches are printed in T.H. Hartley (ed.), *Proceedings of the Parliaments of Elizabeth I*, vols 1 and 2 (Leicester, 1995).

The fullest description of Mary's exile in England can be found in John Daniel Leader, *Mary Queen of Scots in Captivity* (Sheffield, 1880). For Mary's embroidery see the excellent Margaret H. Swain, *The Needlework of Mary, Queen of Scots* (New York and London, 1973). A. Lang, 'The Household of Mary Queen of Scots in 1573', in *Scottish Historical Review* (1905), pp. 345–55, lists the members of Mary's household and points to her generosity towards them.

For political events in Scotland see Ian B. Cowan, 'The Marian Civil War 1567–73' in Norman Macdougall (ed.), *Scotland and War AD 79–1918* (Edinburgh, 1991), pp. 95–108.

The best discussion of the parliamentary debates on Mary remains the two volumes of J.E. Neale, *Elizabeth I and Her Parliaments* (London, 1953–7). His work can be supplemented with G. Bowler, 'An "Axe or an Act": The Parliament of 1572 and Resistance Theory in Early Elizabethan England', *Canadian Journal of History* 19 (1984), pp. 349–59; and Patrick Collinson, 'The Elizabethan Exclusion Crisis' in his *Elizabethan Essays* (London, 1994).

Elizabeth's negotiations can be traced in Mary Patricia Basing, 'Robert Beale and the Queen of Scots', *British Library Journal* 20, (1994), pp. 65–82.

Drawing of Mary's funeral procession, 1587 by an unknown artist. On Sunday 30 July 1587 a procession escorted Mary's embalmed body from Fotheringhay Castle to Peterborough Cathedral, where she was to be buried. Her tomb lay in an aisle opposite that of the dowager queen Katherine of Aragon. (British Library, Additional MS 35324, f. 14)

P.J. Holmes assesses the danger from Mary to Elizabeth in 'Mary Stewart in England' printed in M. Lynch's *Mary Stewart* (1988), though in my view he underestimates it.

Spanish policy towards Mary and England is discussed in Geoffrey Parker, *The Grand Strategy of Philip II* (New Haven, 1998), and is particularly useful on the Ridolfi plot. For reactions to Mary's death in France see Alexander S. Wilkinson, *Mary Queen of Scots and French Public Opinion 1542–1600* (Basingstoke, 2004), pp. 103–56.

Chronology

1542	(24 Nov)	Defeat of the Scots at Solway Moss
	(8 Dec)	Mary's birth
	(14 Dec)	James V's death
1543	(1 July)	Signing of the Treaties of Greenwich (Mary's marriage to Prince Edward)
	(9 Sept)	Mary's coronation
	(11 Dec)	Repudiation of the Treaties of Greenwich
1544	(May)	Beginning of 'Rough Wooing'
1548	(15 Aug)	Mary's arrival in France
1550	(19 Sept)	Beginning of Marie de Guise's year-long visit to France
1558	(April)	Mary's betrothal and marriage to the dauphin, François
1559	(July)	Death of Henri II and accession of François II
	(11 June)	Death of Marie de Guise
	(5 Dec)	Death of François II
1561	(19 Aug)	Mary's arrival in Scotland
1562	(Aug)	Mary's progress in the Highlands
	(28 Oct)	Battle of Corrichie
1563–4		Matrimonial negotiations
1565	(17 Feb)	Mary's meeting with Lord Henry Darnley at Wemyss
	(29 Jul)	Mary's marriage to Henry
	(Aug–Sept)	Chase-about Raid
1566	(9 Mar)	Murder of David Rizzio
	(19 June)	Birth of Prince James
	(15/16 Oct)	Mary's ride from Jedburgh to Hermitage Castle
	(17 Oct)	Mary's illness at Jedburgh
	(20 Nov)	The meeting of Mary's counsellors at Craigmillar Castle
	(17 Dec)	Baptism of James
	(24 Dec)	Pardon of Morton and the other murderers of Rizzio
1567	(22 Jan)	Mary's arrival in Glasgow to see Henry
	(10 Feb)	Assassination of Henry at Kirk o' Field
	(12 Apr)	Bothwell's trial and acquittal
	(24 Apr)	Mary's abduction
	(15 May)	Mary's marriage to Bothwell
	(15 June)	The engagement of Mary's army and the rebels at Carberry Hill
	(17 June)	Mary's imprisonment at Lochleven
	(24 July)	Mary's enforced abdication
	(29 July)	Coronation of James VI

	(22 Aug)	Moray's installation as regent
1568	(2 May)	Mary's escape from Lochleven
	(13 May)	Battle of Langside
	(16 May)	Mary's arrival at Workington in Cumberland
	(17 May)	Mary's move to Carlisle Castle
	(15 July)	Mary's move to Bolton Castle
	(4 Oct)	Opening of tribunal at York to hear the case against Mary
	(25 Nov)	Resumption of tribunal in London
1569	(10 Jan)	Inconclusive outcome to tribunal
	(26 Jan)	Mary's move to Tutbury Castle
	(20 Apr)	Mary's arrival at Wingfield Manor
	(25 May)	Mary's short stay at Chatsworth
	(25 Nov)	Mary's return to Tutbury
	(11 Oct)	The Earl of Norfolk's dispatch to the Tower of London
	(Nov)	The Northern Rebellion
	(25 Nov)	Mary's move to Coventry
1570	(2 Jan)	Mary's return to Tutbury
	(23 Jan)	Assassination of Moray
	(May)	Mary's departure from Tutbury
1571		The Ridolfi plot
1583	(Apr)	Negotiations for Mary's restoration
	(Nov)	Discovery of the Throckmorton plot
1584	(Aug)	Appointment of Sir Ralph Sadler as Mary's custodian
	(Nov)	Debate on the Bond of Association in parliament
1585	(Jan)	Mary's return to Tutbury
	(Apr)	Arrival of Sir Amyas Paulet at Tutbury
	(24 Dec)	Mary's removal to Chartley Hall
1586	(17 July)	Mary's letter to Anthony Babington
	(11 Aug)	Beginning of Mary's two-week stay at Tixall Hall
	(21 Sep)	Mary's move to Fotheringhay from Chartley
	(14 Oct)	Opening of Mary's trial
	(25 Oct)	Reconvening of court in Star Chamber: guilty verdict
	(4 Dec)	Proclamation declaring sentence of death
1587	(1 Feb)	Death warrant signed by Elizabeth
	(3 Feb)	Decision by Elizabeth's council to dispatch warrant to Fotheringhay
	(8 Feb)	Mary's execution

Index